With these insightful meditations upon the Beatitudes, Richard Hipps serves up Christian wisdom born out of transforming encounters with the stuff of real life. Filled with illuminating examples from life, literature, and film, the writer explores how the Beatitudes offer to everyone a profound sense of well-being—if we will only take them to heart. Read it, and be drawn more deeply into the fullness of God.

G. Lee Ramsey, Jr., Memphis Theological Seminary, author of *Preachers and Misfits, Prophets and Thieves: The Minister in Southern Fiction*

THE FOCUSED LIFE

THE BEATITUDES FOR EVERYDAY LIVING

Richard S. Hipps

iUniverse, Inc.
New York   Bloomington

The Focused Life
The Beatitudes for Everyday Living

iUniverse books may be ordered through booksellers or by contacting:

iUniverse
1663 Liberty Drive
Bloomington, IN 47403
www.iuniverse.com
1-800-Authors (1-800-288-4677)

Because of the dynamic nature of the Internet, any Web addresses or links contained in this book
may have changed since publication and may no longer be valid. The views expressed in this work
are solely those of the author and do not necessarily reflect the views of the publisher, and the
publisher hereby disclaims any responsibility for them.

ISBN: 978-1-4401-8088-0 (pbk)
ISBN: 978-1-4401-8090-3 (cloth)
ISBN: 978-1-4401-8089-7 (ebook)

Printed in the United States of America

iUniverse rev. date: 11/19/09

Patricia, when I die they will find your name written on my heart.

CONTENTS

ACKNOWLEDGMENTS

Of the countless persons who helped make this book possible, one deserves special attention: the late Mr. Charles Goodman, a man who encouraged his pastor in more ways than one.

I am also grateful for the staff and members of Trinity Baptist Church, Cordova, Tennessee, who keep me wanting to live the focused life. You truly are my *favorites*.

INTRODUCTION

WAKE UP!

I want to ask you a question, a very personal question. How many happy, healthy, holy Christians do you know? Bet you can count them on the fingers of one hand. Bet you don't even count yourself.

In thirty-five years of Christian ministry, as both a parish minister and a seminary professor, I have met few who feel that they are even close to reaching their full potential as followers of Jesus Christ. It is my prayer that things are about to change, at least for those who read this book. In the pages that follow, I want to challenge you to be more open than ever to the life-changing power of God's word.

In these eight beatitudes, found in Jesus' Sermon on the Mount, we're going to discover everything we need to be vibrant, growing Christians. The word "blessed" used throughout the beatitudes is rendered "happy" in many translations. However, the deepest meaning of the word suggests *a profound sense of well-being.*

But before we dive into our study of the beatitudes, we must prepare our hearts and minds to receive their message. There is ground to clear, rocks to be removed, and soil to be prepared. Here are three necessary preconditions to our study of the beatitudes:

WE MUST LEARN TO SEE DEEPLY

In his wonderful book, *Holy Clues: The Gospel According to Sherlock Holmes*,[1] Stephen Kendrick discusses a short story called "A Scandal in Bohemia." In this story, Sherlock Holmes performs his favorite trick, one that appears in many other stories as well. Dr. Watson, Sherlock Holmes' faithful assistant, has just arrived at 221–B Baker Street, London, where Holmes makes his residence.

Holmes deduces from Dr. Watson's appearance, clothing, and shoes that his friend has been walking in the country, has a careless servant girl, and has returned to practicing medicine. After Holmes carefully details how he picked up all the little clues, Dr. Watson laughs at him and says, "When I hear you give your reasons, the thing always appears to me so ridiculously simple that I could easily do it myself, though at each successive instance of your reasoning I am baffled until you explain your process. And yet, I believe my eyes are as good as yours." Sherlock Holmes agrees with Dr. Watson and then makes a profound statement: "You see, Dr. Watson, *but you do not observe.*"

Next, Sherlock Holmes challenges Dr. Watson to state how many steps lead to his door, steps Dr. Watson has climbed hundreds of times. "How many, Dr. Watson?" "I don't know," answers Dr. Watson. "Quite so," replies Holmes. "You have not observed and yet you have seen. That's just my point." The answer turns out to be seventeen steps, a relatively insignificant fact, it seems, but Sherlock Holmes is suggesting that all of us must learn to *observe* our world in just such a clear way.

So many spiritual experiences, beckonings, intuitions, and miracles are happening every day, but we don't have eyes to see them, let alone benefit from them. We see but we don't see *deeply.* True spirituality is a matter of seeing deeply, not merely affirming a set of doctrines. It is one thing to believe and affirm doctrines about God; it is another thing to experience God deeply.

This leads to the second precondition to our study of the beatitudes:

---

1   Stephen Kendrick, *Holy Clues: The Gospel According to Sherlock Holmes* (New York: Pantheon, 1999), 24–25.

WE MUST APPROACH SCRIPTURE
WITH A BEGINNER'S MIND

It is hard to learn something we think we already know. Most of us carry around a heavy load of preconceptions and presumptions about the scripture, and it is almost impossible to wean ourselves from this very limited perspective.

As we begin our study of the beatitudes, I'm going to ask you to throw away all your preconceived notions of what Jesus taught in this part of his Sermon on the Mount. I want you to start afresh as if you've never read the beatitudes before. Empty your mind and take nothing for granted.

Many Christians read the Bible, but they rarely do so with a clear and uncluttered mind. When they read, they usually do so with the traditional church doctrines of their denomination ringing in the back of their minds. Thus, they are not reading the Bible as it is. They are reading it as they have been conditioned and indoctrinated to read it.

As a young minister, I preached against women in ministry mainly because I had never interpreted the Bible for myself. I read scripture, but with the eyes of my fundamentalist tradition, the eyes of my mentors, the eyes of the preachers I respected. I now read the Bible with my own eyes. I want you to do the same.

I remember reading the testimony of a young man who transferred to Wheaton College from a rigid fundamentalist college.[2] As you probably know, Wheaton is a very conservative college but it is not rigidly fundamentalist. One of Wheaton's professors asked the new student about his previous educational experience:

> "Tony, how does Wheaton differ from your other educational experience?"

> "Well, to tell you the truth, it's a breath of fresh air," he said.

---

2   This story comes from Robert E. Webber's *Evangelicals on the Canterbury Trail* (Waco, TX: Word Books, 1985), 80.

"How so?" the professor responded with curiosity.

"I'm allowed to think here."

"What do you mean?" the professor asked, his curiosity growing by the second.

"In my Bible classes at the other college I began to question some of the interpretations of the institution. I simply wanted answers to some very honest questions about why we believe and practice certain things. The answers I was getting were not satisfactory. So I pushed harder."

"You challenged the professor?"

"Right. I don't think I was obnoxious about it. But apparently the teacher felt the questions were evidence that I was falling away from the truth."

"Why, what happened?"

"He called me into his office for a special session."

"Yes."

"He said, 'Tony, I'm really worried about you. You seem to be slipping spiritually. I'd like to have prayer with you and ask God to get hold of your life again.'"

"And how did you interpret that?"

"It was obvious to me and clear from our conversation that questioning was unacceptable. What is truly spiritual is believing what you are told. A questioning spirit is a doubting spirit and a doubting spirit comes from an unbelieving heart. That's what it boils down to."[3]

Sadly, this kind of conversation is repeated hundreds of times not just in college settings, but also in many local churches. A spirituality

3   Ibid.

of right belief can become, as it did for this college student, a stifling experience, an experience of not being allowed to show some healthy doubt about the faith or its particular denominational interpretation.

Listen carefully to what I am about to say. So many of us who call ourselves "believers" are really believers in our own personal belief systems. Our faith is not really in God but in a substitute, a creation of our mind—an intellectualized image of God. By being willing to give that up, throwing it away, we'll open ourselves up to the possibility of a fresh encounter with God, to a mystery that rises above all rational systems and easy answers.

The third and final precondition to our study of the beatitudes is:

WE MUST WAKE UP

Most people are asleep. They come to this world asleep, they live asleep, they marry asleep, they raise families asleep, and they die asleep. Billions have come to Earth and have slept through the whole process. True spirituality means waking up.

What does it take to wake us up? Some, the fortunate ones, are awakened by the harsh realities of life. We suffer so much that we wake up. Others, sadly, just go on suffering in their sleep and then die. The following story by Anthony De Mello explains well what waking up is like:

> It's like the tramp in London who was settling in for the night. He had hardly been able to get a crust of bread to eat.
>
> Then he reaches this embankment on the river Thames. There was a slight drizzle, so he huddled in his old tattered coat.
>
> He was about to go to sleep when suddenly a chauffeur-driven Rolls-Royce pulls up. Out of the car steps a beautiful young lady who says to him, "My poor

man, are you planning to spend the night here on this embankment?"

And the homeless man says, "Yes." She says, "I won't have it. You are coming to my house and you're going to spend a comfortable night and you're going to get a good dinner."

She insists on his getting in the car and he does. They ride several miles out of London and get to the place where she has a sprawling mansion with large grounds.

They are ushered in by the butler, to whom she says, "James, please make sure he's placed in the visitor's quarters and treated well.

Late in the evening the young lady decides to visit her guest and taps lightly on the door, opens it, and finds the man awake.

She asks, "Did you have a good meal?" The man said, "I never had a better meal in my life, lady."

"Are you warm enough?" He says, "Yes, lovely warm bed."

Then she says, "Do you mind if I sit on the edge of the bed and talk to you?"

He says, "No," and as he scoots over to make room for her, he falls right into the Thames river.[4]

Wake up, friend! It is time to exchange our illusions for reality. There is nothing in this life as important as waking up. Nothing. Socrates said, "The unexamined life is not worth living," but De Mello said, "The unaware life is not worth living."

---

4 Anthony De Mello, *Awareness: The Perils and Opportunities of Reality* (New York: Image Books, 1990), 32–33.

As we examine the beatitudes, may each of us see deeply, approach the scriptures with a beginner's mind, and awaken from our sleep.

CHAPTER ONE

Will the Real You Please Stand Up?

Blessed are the poor in spirit, for theirs is the kingdom of heaven.

—Matthew 5:3

Imagine you are Marlo Morgan, a medical doctor who has been invited to Australia to help write training material and teach in the socialized health care system of that country.

After arriving in Australia, you are pleased to find out that you have been invited to an aboriginal tribal meeting. Waiting outside your five-star hotel, you are surprised when your driver arrives in a topless jeep. You are even more surprised when this thirty-year-old aborigine driver simply says, "Come on!"

What follows is beyond your wildest imagination. Thinking you are going to a two-hour meeting, you are dressed accordingly. However, at this point, you have no idea that you won't return for three months.

In her imaginative book of autobiographical fiction, *Mutant Message Down Under*, Marlo Morgan chronicles her experiences in the Australian bush.[5] It is a spiritual adventure from which we could all learn. Let me tell you some of the things that happened to her.

---

5 See Marlo Morgan's *Mutant Message Down Under* (New York: Harper Perennial, 1991).

After being picked up at the hotel, she was driven for several hours into the bush area of Australia. There she met a tribe of aborigines, none of whom could speak a word of English. Only her driver, Ooota, knew the language.

Stepping out of the jeep, she was told by Ooota that before she could enter the tribe's sacred area, she would have to undergo a purification rite. "Take off your clothes," said Ooota, "and put on this piece of cloth."

Morgan couldn't believe what she was being asked to do. Ooota continued, "Remove everything but the garment I'm giving you. Take off your shoes, hose, undergarments, jewelry, even the bobby pins in your hair."

Then she was taken to an open-pit fire burning near where she had disrobed. She was instructed to step across the pit through the smoke, which was rising up to the heavens. Passing through the smoke was an important part of the purification process.

Then the most unusual thing, something she never expected, happened. A tribal woman approached the fire carrying all of Morgan's possessions in her hands: her clothes; her purse (containing her passport, checkbook, and credit cards); her jewelry (two rings and an expensive diamond watch); and she threw everything into the fire. Marlo was beside herself, as you can imagine. One of those rings was a family heirloom given to her by her Aunt Nola.

But this was just the beginning. As a couple of tribe members put out the fire, Ooota approached Marlo, standing there in her ceremonial dress, and said, "Come, we are leaving now."

"Where are we going?" she inquired.

"On a walkabout."

"Where are you walking to?"

"Across Australia."

"Great! How long will this take?"

"Approximately three full changes of the moon."

"Are you saying walk for three months?"

"Yes, three months more or less."

And walk they did. The book is a powerful, fictional story of the spiritual transformation that a Western woman experienced while living with a "primitive" aboriginal tribe. Of the many lessons she learned, one stands out above the others. The aboriginal people believed that either fear or faith would dominate our life.

Things, they think, generate fear. The more things you have, the more you have to fear. Eventually you are living your life for things and are continually fearful of losing those things. How does all this relate to the words of Jesus in Matthew 5:3, "Blessed are the poor in spirit"? Let us consider the following:

IN THIS WORLD, NOTHING LASTS

Think about this. Sometime in the future someone else will have your job. Someone else will be living in your house. Someone else will be driving your car. And, perhaps, someone else will be married to your spouse.

If you stop long enough to examine your life and its present difficulties, you will discover an important truth. You suffer, and create suffering for others, largely because of things you want or things you desire. It is tough knowing that when we do get what we desire, it cannot and will not last. There is always fear lurking in us because we know deep down that all things are impermanent and will eventually be taken from us.

Nearly every great religious tradition teaches that the secret to happiness is to live fully in the present and to appreciate what one has. "Who is rich?" the Jewish Talmud asks. "He who is contented with his lot." Buddha taught his disciples that the cause of suffering is excessiveness of desire. A wise person once said, "That man is richest whose pleasures are cheapest." It therefore seems that our life's work, spiritually, is to stop wanting to make the impermanent permanent. Let's be honest with ourselves. The reason most of us are unhappy is because we did not get something we wanted, or something came our way that we did not want.

In this first beatitude, Jesus is teaching us that embracing a "poverty of spirit" is not only the work of a lifetime but also the foundation of our spiritual life. What is poverty of spirit? It is detachment, nonpossessiveness, nonclinging. It is recognizing that life's great illusion is mistaking the impermanent for the permanent. Like Jesus, instead of clinging to and trying to manipulate an impermanent existence, we should voluntarily surrender to that which is permanent; namely, the kingdom of God.

ONLY ONE PART OF US IS ETERNAL

Traditional Christian theology teaches that we humans are complex beings composed of three parts: body, soul (psyche), and spirit. Of these three, only the spirit is permanent. Our body and soul form our personality or ego, which is impermanent.

Sadly, our ego (body/soul) has been warped and wounded by the circumstances of life, and this wounded ego, this false self, this *flesh* as the Bible calls it, comes into conflict with our true self, our spiritual nature. Listen to how the scriptures describe this conflict:

> *So I say, live by the spirit* (true self), *and you will not gratify the desires of the sinful nature* (false self).

> *For the sinful nature* (false self) *desires what is contrary to the spirit* (true self), *and the spirit* (true self) *what is contrary to the sinful nature* (false self). *They are in conflict with each other, so that you do not do what you want.*

> *But if you are led by the spirit* (true self), *you are not under law.* (Galatians 5:16–18)

When our spirit or true self is in control, our body and soul (psyche) take their rightful place as servants of the spirit. As mentioned earlier, our lifelong challenge is to grow spiritually, ensuring that the ego, the false self or old man, the impermanent self, becomes the servant of the spirit (true self).

The new man must rule the old man, as the Apostle Paul argued:

> *Now the works of the flesh* (old man) *are evident, which are: adultery, fornication, uncleanness, lewdness, idolatry, sorcery, hatred, contentions, jealousies, outbursts of wrath, selfish ambitions, dissensions, heresies, envy, murders, drunkenness, revelries, and the like;*
>
> *Of such I tell you beforehand, just as I also told you in time past, that those who practice such things will not inherit the kingdom of God.*
>
> *But the fruit of the spirit* (new man) *is love, joy, peace, patience, kindness, goodness, faithfulness, gentleness, and self-control.*
>
> *Against such there is no law.*
>
> *And those who are Christ's have crucified the flesh* (old man) *with its passions and desires.*
>
> *If we live in the spirit* (new man) *let us also walk in the spirit* (new man). (Galatians 5:19–25)

Why is this struggle necessary? Because the flesh, the false self, the old man desires to live forever and control every aspect of our life. But this is part of the *great illusion*. Everything in this world is impermanent, changing, and passing away. Nothing of the old man will survive physical death. Only the new man survives physical death, because that is all that is permanent about us.

Another way to understand this is to see yourself as a combination of a small "i" and a big "I." You have to deny the small "i" in order for the big "I" to direct your life.[6] The small "i" knows itself and feeds itself by comparing itself to others, competing with others, and trying to control others. What motivates small "i" living is *comparison*, *competition*, and *control*.

Big "I" living is totally different. It operates solely in the arena of love because God is love. Made in God's image, we too, at our core, are pure love. We can always tell whether we are living out of the little "i" or the big "I." How? If we are comparing, competing, or trying to control others, we are living out of the little "i."

On the other hand, if we are living a life of love, we are living out of the big "I," reflecting the kind of love described by the Apostle Paul:

> Love suffers long and is kind
> Love does not envy
> Love does not parade itself
> Or is not puffed up
> Love does not behave rudely
> Love does not seek its own
> Love is not easily provoked
> Love thinks no evil
> Love does not rejoice in iniquity
> But rejoices in truth
> Love bears all things, believes all things,
> *Hopes all things, endures all things.* (I Corinthians 13:4–7)

This is big "I" living at its best. Is most of *your* life lived out of little "i" or big "I"?

WE MUST SAY AN EMPHATIC "NO" TO OUR FALSE SELF

Identification with our false self is the root of most of the discontentedness we have experienced in life. Remember, the false self, the little "i," the old man, is made up of what we have, what we do, and what others think of us. Only poverty of spirit will free us from this *great illusion*.

---

6   I am indebted to Richard Rohr, *Everything Belongs* (New York: Crossroad Publishing, 1999).

When our Lord Jesus was tempted by Satan in the wilderness to create a false self, Satan was met with an emphatic "no." Jesus knew that his true identity was not determined by what he had, or what he did, or by what others thought of him. He was who the Father said he was: *"My beloved Son in whom I am well pleased"* (Mark 1:11).[7]

Poverty of spirit is the key to seeing clearly; to shifting our perception so that we experience the kingdom of Heaven in the here and now as Jesus clearly saw it and experienced it. How life would change if you related to my true self out of your own true self. How our lives with God would change if we quit trying to relate to God with our false selves. God is only interested in a relationship with the true self—yours and mine.

This will happen only when we recognize that in this world nothing lasts, that only one part of us is eternal, and we must say an emphatic "no" to the flesh, the old man, the little "i."

---

7   Henri J.M. Nouwen, *Life of the Beloved: Spiritual Living in a Secular World* (New York: Crossroad Publishing, 1992), 29-39.

CHAPTER TWO

The Sweet Struggle

Blessed are those who mourn, for they will be comforted.

—Matthew 5:4

One of the most quoted books of the last twenty-five years is M. Scott Peck's *The Road Less Traveled*. Here is what he says about pain:

> The quickest way to change your attitudes toward pain is to accept the fact that everything that happens to you has been designed for spiritual growth.[8]

That's an incredible statement; that even pain and suffering are designed to further our spiritual growth. Peck seems to imply that we are not bodies that happen to have spirits; rather, we are spiritual beings who happen to have bodies. We are here in the material universe for one purpose and one purpose only: to grow spiritually. And pain is a big part of the process.

That's hard for us to accept but it's true nonetheless. We're like the little first-grade boy I read about who lived in Kentucky. On the first day of school when he had been there for half a day, he started packing up his supplies, getting ready to go home. The teacher said to the little

---

8   M. Scott Peck, *Further Along The Road Less Traveled* (New York: Simon & Schuster, 1993), 24.

boy, "Billy, what are you doing?" and the little boy said, "It's lunch time. It's time to go home."

The teacher then tried to explain, "Well, Billy, you're in the first grade now. In kindergarten you only stayed a half a day, but now in the first grade we eat lunch at school and stay all day." The little boy thought about it for a second and said, "Well, who in the heck signed me up for that?"[9] That may be exactly how we feel about pain and suffering. Who in the heck signed us up for that?

GOD'S WAKE UP CALL

Those who take the Bible seriously know that suffering is an essential part of the human condition, one of the engines of spiritual development. It is only when adversity has knocked down our defenses that we ask the important questions: *Who am I? Who is God? What is my purpose for being here?*

I have never known anyone to ask these questions without being forced to do so. Hard times *make* us ask the hard questions. That's why suffering is beneficial. It awakens us spiritually. That's why Jesus said, "Blessed (happy) are those who mourn." Why? Because pain is the greatest wake-up call.

Never think suffering is a waste of time. Something wonderful and positive happens alongside our pain and misery if we choose to see it. This is God's plan for our spiritual well-being. I would have never been awakened to the purpose of my life had it not been for the suffering that came my way. You see, suffering begins the journey to wisdom.

When I was twenty years old I was jarred into life by death, my mother's death. Up until that time my life had been mechanical, unthinking, and routine. Then, all of a sudden, the bottom dropped out of my world. I learned early that there is no coming to spiritual consciousness without pain. Pain is the activator that forces us to choose between what is important and what is not.

---

9   R. Scott Colglazer, *Circling the Divine: Spiritual Reflections for the Journey* (St. Louis: Chalice Press, 1998), 77.

Robert Urich, the actor, learned much about life when he was diagnosed with cancer. He and his wife, Heather, had just completed building their dream house in Utah. Their teenage kids, Ryan and Emily, were healthy and thriving. In the midst of all these blessings, Robert was diagnosed with synovial cell sarcoma, a very serious and rare form of soft-tissue cancer.

When the producers of his successful television show, *The Lazarus Man*, learned of his illness, they cancelled the series. They were afraid he would die in midseason. He didn't die but recovered and was awakened to life in a new way. Even though he suffered through three surgeries, chemotherapy, and radiation, he reclaimed a powerful love of life that deepened his spiritual beliefs.

When he was cancer-free for a year, he and his wife adopted a beautiful baby girl named Alison. This is something they had wanted to do before Robert's cancer. In an interview, Robert said he had spent the morning rocking his infant daughter on a porch swing for three hours. "Before the cancer I would never have done that. I would have missed this most remarkable experience," he said. "I would have felt the need to be doing something—making phone calls, mowing the lawn, or washing the car."[10]

Like Robert Urich, we will learn to use suffering as an opportunity for change and growth. Jesus is saying in this beatitude that suffering brings riches we can find no other way. Have you ever considered the notion that those vexing dilemmas that plague your life are God's messengers to challenge you to open yourself to new ways of thinking? The difficult things you are facing could be the means by which something mysterious, perhaps even great, will be born in you.

I ALSO BELIEVE IN PAIN

In 1997, I attended a conference in California where I heard John Wimber, founder of the Vineyard movement, give his testimony. If you know anything about John Wimber, you know he wrote several best-

---

10 Kathleen A. Brehony, *After the Darkest Hour: How Suffering Begins The Journey to Wisdom* (New York: Henry Hold & Co., 2000), 58.

selling books on the subject of healing. What he preached was called "Power Evangelism," the belief that the preaching of the gospel should be accompanied by the signs and wonders of healing and deliverance.

At the end of his sermon that day he invited people to come forward for prayer. He said, "We are going to call out several symptoms. If any of these symptoms describe you, please come and tell us." I have always been skeptical of faith healing but that week I was listening with different ears. You see, two days earlier doctors had found a tumor in my right sinus. I was scheduled for surgery in two weeks to determine if the tumor was malignant. I said to myself, "God, I want to believe this. If there's anything to this, let him describe my symptoms."

I sat there listening to every kind of ailment being mentioned: heart problems, arthritis, back pain, and then those words I'll never forget. *"There is someone here who has been told this week that they have a tumor in their right sinus."* I could not believe what I was hearing. Something moved me out of my chair and I went forward. A young man about my son's age came to me and said, "Do you mind if I lay my hand on your chest?" "No, I don't mind. Go ahead," I said. What happened next is incredible.

He told me that the Holy Spirit was revealing that my tumor was benign, that I would be fine, and that I could quit worrying. "Also," he said, "the Holy Spirit says you should rest more." I knew then that what he said came straight from God. Two weeks later I had the surgery and, as this young man had prophesied, the tumor was benign.

John Wimber taught me much that day about believing God for healing. He also taught me something else. He taught me that sometimes the healing comes in ways we don't expect. John Wimber died recently, and during the final five years of his life he suffered through a heart attack, a stroke, and finally, cancer. Two years after being diagnosed with an inoperable tumor he wrote an article called "Signs, Wonders, and Cancer." He ended the article with these words:

While I was being treated for cancer, someone wrote me a letter asking, "Do you still believe in healing now that you've got cancer?" I wrote back: "Yes! I do." And the truth is, I do.

I also believe in pain. Both are found in the Word of God. In the year I spent battling cancer God purged me of a lot of habits and attitudes that weren't right, and through it I grew stronger as a Christian. Some of my greatest spiritual advances in spiritual maturity came as I embraced the pain—as each day I had to choose to allow God to accomplish his work in me by any method, even adversity ...

Going through the valley of the shadow is frightening. Its uncertainties keep you alert to every changing scenario. I began to cling to every nuance of the doctor's words, shrugs, and grimaces; I experienced the full range of emotions that go with the life-threatening illness. I wept as I saw my utter need to depend on God ... I had to embrace the truth that I could not control my life ... I also found that the view from the valley gave me a focus on Christ that I would not have found any other way.[11]

THE CHOICE IS OURS

If you haven't read the book of Habakkuk lately, do so—especially the writer's closing prayer. Habakkuk thought that God had left Israel forever because of Israel's sin. However, he chose to trust anyway, expressing his faith with these timeless words:

Though the fig tree does not bud and there are no grapes on the vines, though the olive crop fails and the fields produce no food, though there are no sheep in the pen

---

11 John Wimber, "Signs, Wonders, and Cancer." *Christianity Today* (October 7, 1996): 49–51.

> *and no cattle in the stalls, yet I will rejoice in the Lord, I*
> *will be joyful in God my savior.* (Habakkuk 3:17–18)

All of us have an important choice to make. We can either suffer foolishly or we can suffer redemptively. If we suffer redemptively we'll be blessed, as Jesus teaches us in this beatitude. In our pain we will come to know God more intimately, because suffering creates a peculiar kind of fellowship with Christ and this is how we're comforted.

Habakkuk *chose* to trust God even when the crops failed and invaders stormed his city. John Wimber *chose* to trust God even in the midst of heart disease and cancer. I *chose* to trust God even if it meant carrying on without my mother and later without my precious little daughter, Alexandra.

The great reformer, Martin Luther, knew that there is sweetness in the struggle when he wrote, "Do not begrudge affliction. It is for your good. Affliction teaches you to experience and understand how faithful, true, and mighty are the comforting words of God." The reformer went on to say, "I myself owe my adversary many thanks for beating and frightening me because these pains have turned me to God … driving me to a goal I would never have reached."[12] You can be sure those whom God uses greatly, suffer greatly. It was true for Jesus and it will be true for us.

I want to conclude by suggesting the following guided mediation.

THE EXCHANGE OF GIFTS

Imagine that you are in a circle of elders. Around you stand older men and women, their beauty sculpted by time. See their flowing gray hair, their warm, wrinkled faces. You, too, stand with them. In the middle of your circle is a cluster of jeweled boxes.

"What is in your box?" someone from the circle calls out. "What is your gift to us?"

---

12 Heiko A. Oberman, *Luther: Man Between God and the Devil* (New Haven, CT: Yale Curiosity Press, 1982), 323.

One man replies, "In the box is a symbol of my blindness. My blindness is my gift. In my old age I have lost my sight. But through this blindness I have been able to see more deeply into others. When I hear your voice I am not distracted by surface appearance. I see your soul in all its beauty. I also sense your pain and fear. And my blindness helps me to understand that as well." Slowly the blind man places his box in the center.

Then another standing in the circle calls out, "This is your gift to all of us. Now tell us, what do you need to receive?"

The blind man replies, "I have need of a trusted companion in life. Someone sighted who can help me across a busy street. Someone to describe the sunset that I'll never see." Then you hear a voice respond, "This shall be supplied." An elder steps forward to hand the blind man a box that another person had left in the center. Inside is a symbol of a trusted companion—just what the blind man needs. With gladness he returns to the outer circle.

Now, one by one, you see others step forth, each person bearing a box. Inside is a symbol of some suffering they have undergone: a broken heart, a disability, a painful loss. But each person describes why this suffering is their gift, how it has deepened their ability to help others. And each person describes also what they need back. Always, the voice responds, "This shall be supplied." Each person is handed the gift left by another in this mystical exchange.

Finally it is your turn. Imagine yourself stepping to the center of the circle. You are surrounded by the wise and compassionate elders. You hear the question,

"What is in your box?" Pause here, and let yourself know. What is the suffering that is your gift to the others? Think about the many ways this source of pain has enabled you to give. How has it made you more understanding, compassionate, open, or skillful? Think of the many people your suffering has enabled you to help. Friends, family members, clients. Hear yourself speak of all this to the elders. Your words may be halting. That's okay. Stay with it. When you are ready, place your box in the center.

Then open yourself to the next question: "And what is it you need to receive?" Your suffering has also left you broken. What is it that you need to make you whole—from other people, from yourself, from Spirit? Let your answer well up from your heart. Speak of it to the elders. Take your time. Don't be afraid to ask for all you need.

When you are ready, hear the response, "It shall be supplied." Imagine an elder stepping forward to hand you a box containing all that you need. Think on ways this support has already come true in your life. What are some gifts you've received from others—love, companionship, assistance—that have helped you in your suffering? When has God or Spirit been present to see you through? Also know that much in your box has yet to be revealed. But as you age, you will be taken care of. What you need shall be supplied.[13]

I want you to think about this visualization in the days to come. Return to it mentally again and again. When you have suffering, you can visualize placing it in a box as a gift to others. And, you can remember that there is another box that has within it all that you need. Don't be afraid to open it.

---

13 Drew Leder, *Spiritual Passages: Embracing Life's Saved Journey* (New York, Penguin Putnam, 1997), 243.

CHAPTER THREE

Meek Is Not Weak

Blessed are the meek, for they will inherit the earth.

—Matthew 5:5

Some movies feed your soul. In fact, the gospel message is presented more clearly in some films than it is from some pulpits. Take the movie *Bambi,* for instance. Until 1970 it was the most successful film in history. What does *Bambi* teach us theologically?

Let's consider one scene in particular. It is a scene in which the peace of the forest is disturbed by a sudden panic. Startled deer scurry everywhere, fleeing from what, we don't know. Then we hear the crack of a rifle. After Bambi and his mother are at a safe distance, the little fawn asks, "What happened, Mother? Why did they all run?" She pauses a moment before she answers. "Man ... was in the forest."

Before you know it, you are looking at Man from the perspective of a little deer. C.S. Lewis once wrote, "Each of us by nature sees the whole world from one point of view with a perspective and selectiveness peculiar to himself."[14] *Bambi* (the movie and the book) helps us

---

14 See Ken Gire's *Reflections on the Movies* (Colorado Springs, CO: Chariot Victor Books, 2000) 61.

transcend our nature, allowing us to hear with other ears, see with other eyes, and feel with other hearts.

The true beginning of our growth as a human being is the ability to step out of ourselves and see the world through someone else's eyes. In the story of *Bambi*, several of the animals had seen Man in the forest, but no one could explain him. No animal could explain how Man could kill from such a great distance, though each had a theory.

Listen to the animals:

> Bambi's mother said, "He throws his hand at you, my grandmother told me."
>
> "Is that so?" asked old Nettla. "What is it that bangs so terribly then?"
>
> "That's when he tears his hand off," Bambi's mother explained. "Then the fire flashes and the thunder cracks. He's all fire inside."
>
> "Excuse me," said Ronno. "It's true that he's all fire inside. But that about his hand is wrong. A hand couldn't make such wounds. You can see that for yourself. It's much more likely that it's a tooth he throws at us. A tooth would explain a great many things, you know. You really die from his bite."
>
> "Will he never stop hunting us?" Young Karus sighed.
>
> Then Marena spoke, the young half-grown doe. "They say that sometime he'll come to live with us and be as gentle as we are. He'll play with us then and the whole forest will be happy, and we'll be friends with him."[15]

---

15 Ibid., 63.

BLESSED ARE THE GENTLE

What did Jesus mean when He said "Blessed are the meek"? Mistakenly, most of us think meek equals weak. Not so! In the original Greek, the word for meek, *praus* is better translated as *gentle*. It conveys the idea of tamed strength, self-control.

You've seen those huge Clydesdale horses that are hitched up to pull great logs out of the forest for timber companies. Clydesdales are so strong yet so gentle that little children can crawl all over them and play at their feet without injury. That's the biblical picture of meekness, tamed strength.[16]

Jesus was a gentle person. Listen to the way He describes Himself in this wonderful invitation:

> *Come to me all ye that labor and are heavy laden,*
> *and I will give you rest.*
> *Take my yoke upon you, and learn of me;*
> *for I am meek and lowly in heart:*
> *and ye shall find rest unto your souls.*
> *For my yoke is easy, and my burden is light.*
> (Matthew 11:28–30)

Do you remember how gently Jesus treated the adulterous woman who had been thrown at his feet by the Pharisees? He didn't shame her by describing her lifestyle. He didn't remind her of the scriptures she was violating. He didn't put her down for being less than perfect.

A writer, Michael Yaconelli, loves this story so much that he decided to put himself in it as a member of the crowd—just an ordinary observer. Here is his imaginary description of what happened:

> I left the crowd early. I didn't think I could stomach
> a stoning. I had seen too many in my lifetime, but I
> was intrigued with this Jesus person. I circled around to
> watch, as one by one each person left the woman, until
> she was standing alone. I will never forget the look on

---

16 Stephen M. Crotts, *The Beautiful Attitudes* (Lima, OH: CSS Publishing, 1996), 31.

her face—distant, blank, no defiance left in her. It was obvious she had given up. Her shoulders were slumped forward, her face looked old, deep lines of pain etched upon it. She was not humiliated by this experience; she was beyond humiliation. She was no stranger to the disdain of men. She had suffered abuse before—most of her life, really. Suffering abuse was her companion, her place.

I watched her standing there for what seemed like hours. The silence was deafening—you could actually hear the footsteps of those leaving. She just stood there with Jesus. He had knelt down while all of this was happening, writing in the sand. She looked straight ahead, ignoring Him, ignoring all of us, but when everyone had left I could see her look ever so slightly first to the left and then to the right. When she realized she was alone, I could see the amazed look on her face. She couldn't believe it! All of her accusers were gone! I swear to you, it looked as if the wrinkles on her face suddenly disappeared. Her eyes, no longer dull and colorless, seemed to flash in the desert sun. She looked at Him for the first time, trying to take Him all in, trying to understand this strange man who acted like no man she had ever met. He said something to her. I couldn't hear what He said, but I did notice the tears. They came slowly at first then drowned her face in a lifetime of sorrow. She cried a long time, as though her soul were cleansing itself.

I will never forget what Jesus did next. He stood facing her, staring intently at her tear-soaked face. She was standing much straighter, her shoulders upright and strong. He reached down to her and gently, tenderly, wiped the tears from her face. She stopped crying. He cupped her face in His hands and bent down and kissed her on the forehead. He held her face a very long time, not really looking at her but through her, as though He were looking at her heart, at all the scars on her soul. It was as if He was healing her soul, looking her sin away. And then, abruptly, he let go of her face, turned to leave, turned back, and ... winked.[17]

ARE YOU A GENTLE PERSON?

Would you consider yourself a gentle person? In your day-to-day life do you demonstrate a mild disposition, a temperate, considerate spirit? In our lifetime we have all known gentle people. The moment you enter the space of a gentle person, you feel a wonderful influence. You feel positive, elevated, inspired.

There is an interesting retired couple living in New York City. They demonstrate the spirit of gentleness so well. Each day they play what they call "the Lift Game." They try to give a lift to people by showing kindness wherever they go—be it a store clerk, a taxi driver, a building doorman. They simply try to affirm people by being kind. Then, in the evening when they are having dinner together, they talk about the "lifts" they gave to people during the day. By practicing gentleness and kindness, this couple became a medium for God's goodwill toward humanity. They deliberately entered into a partnership with God's positive forces at work in the universe.

Philippians 4:5 tells us, *Let your gentleness be evident to all.* Colossians 3:12 adds, *Clothe yourselves with gentleness.* Paul is even more direct in I Timothy 6:11, telling us to "pursue" gentleness. Even wayward Christians are to be nurtured back into fellowship by gentleness. Paul counseled in Galatians 6:1, *If someone is caught in a sin, you who are spiritual should restore him gently.* Even though someone has perhaps brought shame on the name of Christ, we are urged to reach out to that person in a spirit of gentleness.

---

17 Michael Yaconelli, *Dangerous Wonder* (Colorado Springs, CO: Navpress, 1998), 133.

CULTIVATING A SPIRIT OF GENTLENESS

Never equate gentleness with weakness. It takes great strength and tremendous spiritual fortitude to become a gentle soul. In the movie *The War*, Kevin Costner plays a Vietnam vet who is scarred deeply from his experience in Southeast Asia. His goal in life has now become making the world better than he found it. Sadly, conflict continues to plague him when he returns home. Neighborhood bullies are constantly harassing his two children.

In one scene, Costner is buying cotton candy for his wife and daughter, not realizing that the bullies are beating up his son once more. Later, as Costner is escorting his son to the family car, he sees two of the bullies who have been picking on his children. He walks over to them and offers them the cotton candy, which they hesitatingly accept. The bullies are not sure what he's doing, but the lure of the candy is irresistible.

Costner's ten-year-old son is enraged. "Do you know who they are? They're the kids who beat me up!" "I know that," his dad calmly replies. "Then why did you give them the candy?" the boy asks. He answers, "Because they look like they haven't been given anything in a long time." The movie goes on to show that the son develops the kindness and gentleness displayed by his father. It changes his life completely, culminating in a courageous act that transcends all the previous friction.

What's the point? We should treat others as God does. We are His children. We should act as He does. Gentleness and kindness should be given to all because gentleness and kindness have the inherent power to transform lives.

Rosa Parks, a black seamstress from Montgomery, Alabama, is a wonderful example of the strength of gentleness. On December 1, 1955, she was on her way home from work when she climbed onto a bus. At the next stop, a white businessman came onto the bus and the bus driver told Rosa Parks she would have to stand so that he could expand the white seating area.

Rosa Parks later said that all she knew was that she was tired and she gently said, "No," and refused to move. She had no idea that in that same city of Montgomery, God had a preacher named Martin Luther King, Jr. Her simple, gentle, act of conscience sparked a moral reformation that changed the social fabric of America. In this simple act, you see what one gentle person can do.

Think deeply about the beautiful words of Dr. Martin Luther King, Jr, and remind yourself that your objective as a Christian is to live a life of gentleness:

> The nonviolent approach does not immediately change the heart of the oppressor. It first does something to the hearts and souls of those committed to it. It gives them a new self-respect; it calls up resources of strength and courage that they did not know they had. Finally it reaches the opponent and so stirs his conscience that reconciliation becomes a reality.[18]

Dr. King is speaking of something happening to the heart and soul of those who are committed to a life of kindness and gentleness. If we commit ourselves to live from a gentle heart we will behave more courageously and with a strength that we have never known before. When you walk the gentle pathway, your gentleness overwhelms your opponent and so stirs his or her conscience that reconciliation becomes a reality. It happened with Jesus. It will happen with us.

INHERIT THE EARTH

Listen once again to the words of our Lord: *Blessed are the meek, for they will inherit the earth* (Mathew 5:5). This beatitude is a direct quote from Psalm 37:22 where it says, *But the meek (gentle) shall inherit the land, and delight themselves in abundant prosperity.*

---

18 Wayne W. Dyer, *Wisdom of the Ages* (New York: HarperCollins, 1998), 251.

Let's not miss the irony here. In Jesus' day there was one group hated by all the people—the landowners. Those who possessed the land did so by violence and oppression. In his great Sermon on the Mount Jesus was reminding the people that only God owns the land. *The Earth is the Lord's and all that is in it, the world and those who live in it* (Psalm 24:1).

Owning property forces us behind fences, boundaries, and walls. Before long we begin thinking that we actually "own" the ground we live on because there's a deed down at the courthouse. Spiritual people know better. Only God possesses the Earth. We are only stewards of God's Earth.

What do you possess? Wait a few years; when you're six feet under, you'll know. You possess nothing. What you think you possess will actually possess you after a while. Once the gospel message takes root in your life you will know that possessions are a passing illusion. The gentle, the meek, these are the ones to whom the Earth will be given. This beatitude seems illogical, but it's true nonetheless.

METTA MEDITATION

Allow me to challenge you to do something that perhaps you have never done. There is an ancient form of mediation called Metta Meditation that is sometimes described as "gentling the heart."

Metta Meditation suggests that we remember a time when someone treated us with kindness and love, and then allow that feeling of being loved to come alive in us again. Saturating ourselves in that remembrance of love, we may then mentally send that loving kindness to others. Begin with someone close to you and end with the people who have brought you pain. This beautiful form of meditation can be a daily heartfelt wish for the happiness, well-being, and peace of others and ourselves. Here are still other ways to meditate:

- Those who have difficulty finding such a memory with another person might bring to mind that kind of unconditional love from an animal or pet.

- Others might imagine spiritual figures or biblical characters that they admire.

- Nature often sends us kindness and love through the shining warmth of the sun or a soft breeze on our skin. Remember that feeling from some day gone by.

- The *source* of our feeling loved is not important. But the *feeling of being loved is*.[19]

---

19 Diane Berke, *The Gentle Smile* (New York: Crossroads Publishers, 1995), 37.

CHAPTER FOUR

Willing the One Thing

Blessed are those who hunger and thirst for righteousness,
for they will be filled.

—Matthew 5:6

Inside each of us is an unquenchable fire, a restlessness, a loneliness, a longing, a gnawing nostalgia, an all-embracing hunger. This *dis-ease* is universal. Every human being is overcharged with a desire for the divine and this desire is always stronger than any satisfaction.

Ultimately, what we do with this dis-ease, this hunger for the holy, is address it spiritually. It was St. Augustine who said, "You have made us for yourself, Lord, and our hearts are restless until they rest in you." Spirituality is what we do with our unrest.

MOTHER TERESA, JANIS JOPLIN, & PRINCESS DIANA

Our spirituality is either a life-giving spirituality or a life-denying spirituality. The choice is ours. What we do with that unquenchable fire, how we channel it, will determine our spirituality. This is well illustrated by comparing the lives or three very famous women: Mother Teresa, Janis Joplin, and Princess Diana.[20]

First, there's Mother Teresa. None of us would doubt this woman's healthy spirituality. Although she appeared frail and meek, she was a human bulldozer. Channeling the fire within, she was passionately dedicated to God and the poor. Søren Kierkegaard defined a saint as *someone who can will the one thing.* Mother Teresa willed one thing— Jesus Christ. She channeled her fire, her spiritual hunger, in the direction of the only one who could satisfy that hunger.

Janis Joplin, the rock star who died at the age of twenty-seven from a drug overdose, was not all that different from Mother Teresa. She too was an exceptional woman fueled by an unquenchable fire. However, unlike Mother Teresa, Janis Joplin did not will the one thing. She willed many things. Her spiritual energy was dispersed in all directions and eventually she died, spiritually drained. Her fire, her spiritual life force, was depleted by a total abandonment to performance, drugs, and sex. She was like the fig tree that offered no fruit to Jesus:

> *Now in the morning as He returned to the city, He was hungry. And seeing a fig tree by the road, He came to it and found nothing on it but leaves, and said to it, "Let no fruit grow on you ever again." Immediately the fig tree withered away.* (Matthew 21:18–20)

This text has always puzzled me. Why would Jesus curse a fig tree? It seems so out of character for Jesus to curse anything, much less a tree. However, I've come to believe that our Lord cursed this tree not because He was hungry but because it had withheld its life force from Him.

---

20 I am indebted to Ronald Rolheiser. In his book, *The Holy Longing: The Search for A Christian Spirituality*, (New York: Doubleday, 1999), there is a wonderful comparison of Mother Teresa, Janis Joplin, and Princess Diana (pp. 7–11).

In Ezekiel 47, the writer paints a fascinating picture of a stream that begins as a mere trickle in the temple and then grows into a river too wide to swim across:

> *Everything will live where the river goes. There will be trees of many different kinds. And their fruit will be for food, their leaves for healing.* (Ezekiel 47:8–12)

This is also a wonderful description of what occurs when people share their life force, their fire, and their spiritual energy. Their existence on this planet creates an ever-expanding river, teeming with life and possibilities.[21]

Finally, there's Princess Diana. Most of us, spiritually, are more like Princess Diana: half Mother Teresa, half Janis Joplin. Diana channeled her fire, her spiritual life force, in two directions: to the poor *and* to the high life. Remember, spirituality is about what we do with the fire inside us, about how we channel it. Unlike Mother Teresa and Janis Joplin, Princess Diana chose to walk a dual road that led to disintegration and death. She did not heed the words of our Lord:

> *No one can serve two masters; for either he will hate the one and love the other, or else he will be loyal to the one and despise the other. You cannot serve God and mammon.*
> (Matthew 6:24)

Unless we *will the one thing*, unless we seek first the Kingdom of God and His righteousness, unless we hunger and thirst for the holy, we too will end up spiritually bankrupt.

GOD LOOKS FOR THE HUNGRY

In the New Testament, those who were hungry and desperate spiritually forgot niceties and protocol and chased after God with a passion. It was rudeness born out of desperation.

---

21 Laurie Beth Jones, *Jesus in Blue Jeans* (New York: Hyperion Press, 1997), 181–182.

You remember the desperate woman who suffered an incurable hemorrhaging problem. She shoved and elbowed her way through the crowd until she was able to touch the hem of the Lord's garment (Matthew 9:20–21). Then there was that rude Canaanite woman (not even a Jew) who kept begging Jesus to deliver her daughter from demon possession (Matthew 15:22–28). Jesus tested her passion by saying, "It is not good to take the children's bread and throw it to the little dogs" (Matthew 15:26). She passed His test, replying, "Yes, Lord, yet even the little dogs eat the crumbs, which fall from their master's table" (Matthew 15:27). She was so rude, so brash, and so pushy—and Jesus loved it!

What about the four men (Mark 2:1–5) who carried their paralytic friend to Jesus and couldn't reach Him for the crowd? What did they do? They climbed up on the roof, broke through, and lowered the man down to Jesus. Was Jesus upset because they disturbed Him in the middle of His sermon? No, indeed! I believe He laughed out loud and was elated at their audacity.

We don't see this kind of hunger in the church today. Maybe that's why we don't see these kinds of miracles either. God seems drawn to those who hunger and thirst for Him. We need to reacquaint ourselves with some of the most exciting promises in the Bible. Promises like:

> *When you search for me, you will find me, if you seek me with all your heart.* (Jeremiah 29:13)

> *I love those who love me and those who seek me diligently find me.* (Proverbs 8:17)

> *But without faith it is impossible to please Him, for he who comes to God must believe that He is, and that He is a rewarder of those who diligently seek Him.* (Hebrews 11:6)

God is not interested in halfhearted seeking. Only those who are diligent, overeager, zealous, psyched up, are going to find Him in special ways. You don't play with God and get blessed. True seeking is more than feeling good religiously. True seeking engages all of your heart.

True seeking makes this statement to God: "Lord, I mean business with You."

When you are on your knees in prayer, when you are driving to work, when you are having dinner with your family, when you are out on a date, when you are at school, when you are on the Internet, whatever you are doing, you say to God, "Lord, I want a life fully pleasing to You. I seek You diligently in all that I do. Bless me according to the passion with which I seek You."

GOD IS NOT A GENIE

"Aladdin and the Magic Lamp" is a story from *Tales of the Arabian Nights*. It is the story of a boy who found a magic lamp in which resided a generous genie. Aladdin was granted three wishes and the rest is history.

Have you ever thought about the relationship between Aladdin and the genie? It was not a real friendship. They were not bosom buddies. There was not a fondness and a love between them. There was no intimacy. Their only communication was when Aladdin was in trouble or needed something. He didn't love the genie. He *used* the genie to meet his own selfish needs.

Sound familiar? How many of us are guilty of the same selfishness and insensitivity? Sadly, many of us want to use God to meet our own selfish needs. A loving relationship with God is secondary. We only call on God when we're in trouble or need something. How many of us are seeking things from God under the pretense of seeking God? It's not enough just to seek His gifts—we've got to first seek the Giver. It's not enough just to seek God's blessings—we've got to seek the Blesser. We don't need more *things*; we need God.

If we are honest, we will admit that most of the time we are seeking things from God. "I'm sick; heal me. I can't pay my bills; give me money. I'm depressed; make me happy." We call this "seeking God," but it is not.

When you seek God, you are expecting only one thing: God! The prayer of your life should be, "God, I just want You." When is the last time you prayed like that? When is the last time you sought His face instead of His hand? Are you more hungry for the Blesser, or the blessings; the Giver, or the gift?

A WARNING

What happens when we don't seek God with hungry hearts? What happens when we carry on with our Christian routines without the manifest presence of God? I think you know.

Aleksandr Solzhenitsyn, the Russian writer, was a twentieth-century prophet. When he received the Templeton Award in 1983, he began his address with these sobering words:

> Over half a century ago, while I was still a child, I recall hearing a number of older people offer the following explanation for the great disasters that had befallen Russia. "Men have forgotten God; that's why all this has happened." Since then I have spent well-nigh fifty years working on the history of our revolution; in the process I have read hundreds of books, collected hundreds of personal testimonies, and have already contributed eight volumes of my own toward the effort of clearing away the rubble left by that upheaval. But if I were asked today to formulate as concisely as possible the main cause of the ruinous revolution that swallowed up some sixty million of our people, I could not put it more accurately than to repeat: "Men have forgotten God; that's why all this has happened."[22]

When we forget God, when we don't seek God with hungry hearts, bad things are bound to happen. We are left to our own weary and wearisome selves, struggling along with neither power nor peace. Means and methods cannot replace the departed glory. John Owen,

---

22 Aleksandr Solzhenitsyn, "Men Have Forgotten God," *Religion in Communist Dominated Areas* 22 (1983): 54.

a great writer from another generation, advised us, "God will be with us in visible manifestations of His favor, when we are with Him in convincing demonstrations of our seeking."[23]

A little child was playing hide and seek with some of her friends. She had hidden herself well. But while she was hiding, her friends proceeded to sneak home and didn't tell her. After a very long time the little girl realized that no one was looking for her. Her friends had abandoned her. Imagine how she felt. She ran home and threw herself into her daddy's arms and cried, "Daddy, I was hiding and nobody tried to find me!" Her father hugged her close and comforted her with these words, "God understands, baby. He understands more than you realize."[24]

---

23 John Owen, "God's Presence With A People: The Spring of Their Prosperity," in *The Works of John Owen*, ed. Goold, vol. 8, 431–452,

24 Tony Campolo, *Let Me Tell You A Story*, (Nashville: Word Publishing, 2000), 1.

CHAPTER FIVE

Forgiven to Forgive

Blessed are the merciful, for they will be shown mercy.

—Matthew 5:7

Are you one of those people who believe that what goes around comes around? Alexander Fleming certainly was. Years ago, in Scotland, his father was walking by a bog when he heard someone yell, "Help me! Help me! Someone, please help me!" Fleming's father, a poor farmer, ran to where he heard the cry for help and saw a young boy sinking in thick, black muck. With care and skill, he saved the boy from certain death.

The next day a knock was heard at the Flemings' cottage. As the father opened the door, a very wealthy gentleman greeted him. The man had arrived in a stately carriage. The poor farmer was confused as to why someone of such high stature had come to call on him. Soon his question was answered.

"Sir, you saved my son yesterday, and I am here to reward you," spoke the gentleman. The farmer, however, refused to accept the money offered to him. Saving a child's life required no reward. Impressed by Fleming's character, the wealthy gentleman insisted on helping the poor family. Seeing the farmer's young son standing at his side, the wealthy man made a second offer. "Since you helped my son, may I help yours? If you will allow me to take custody of your boy, I will see to it that he receives the finest education available."

The poor man, grateful for the offer, sent his son away with the nobleman. The son became an outstanding student and eventually graduated from St. Mary's Hospital Medical School in London. Because of this wealthy man's gift, the poor farmer's son, in turn, gave a gift to the entire world: He discovered penicillin. The poor farmer's son became Sir Alexander Fleming.

But the story doesn't end there. The nobleman's son's life was threatened for a second time. Now grown, he lay dying of pneumonia. Ironically, it was the poor farmer's son who would save his life a second time when the penicillin was prescribed.

The wealthy nobleman had provided for the education of Sir Alexander Fleming and that education had saved his son. His son's name? Sir Winston Churchill.[25] What goes around does come around. *Whatsoever a man sows, that shall he also reap* (Galatians 6:7). If you sow good things, you reap good things. If you sow bad things, you reap bad things.

In this beatitude Jesus is encouraging us to sow the seeds of mercy and forgiveness generously. Why? Because He knows we all need a bumper crop of the same.

IS GOD *REALLY* MERCIFUL?

Have you ever noticed that those who feel less judged by God tend to be more tolerant of others? They are less judgmental, less critical. Having received God's forgiveness and mercy, they are quick to offer the same to others.

Our concept of God determines the kind of people we become. If we serve an angry God, we will be angry people. If our God keeps a

---

25 H. Jackson Brown, Jr. *Highlighted in Yellow* (Nashville, Rutledge Hill Press, 2001), 11–12.

ledger of wrongs, we will keep a ledger of wrongs. If our God accepts us when we're good and rejects us when we're bad, then we will accept people when they're good and reject them when they're bad. We will treat others the way we think God treats us.

Because of Jesus Christ, we should believe that God is madly in love with us. And yet, sadly, so few of us believe this. It is so hard for us to believe that we are accepted, as we are, forgiven for all of our sins—past, present, and future—and continually cared for by a loving gracious God.

The gospel truth is that God's love and mercy are the only things that can radically reshape our identity. Julian of Norwich wrote, "The greatest honor that we can give to Almighty God is to live gladly because of the knowledge of His love."[26] We have been completely accepted by the one whose acceptance is all that really matters.

In 1 Corinthians 13:4–8 we are given a beautiful description of what God's love toward us is like:

> *Love is patient, love is kind. It does not envy, it does not boast, it is not proud. It is not rude, it is not self-seeking, it is not easily angered, it keeps no record of wrongs. Love does not delight in evil but rejoices with the truth. It always protects, always trusts, always hopes, always perseveres. Love never fails.*

As incredible as it sounds, this is exactly how God loves each and every one of us. He is patient with us—He puts up with our faults and failures. He is kind toward us—He gives us what we need and not what we deserve. He is not boastful—why would He need to boast? He is not rude—He has no need to offend or insult us. He keeps no records of our wrongs—we don't have to fear a future judgment.

God lives by the same standard of love that He asks us to live by. He tells us not to track the wrongs that other people do to us. He tells us not to punish those that harm us. He tells us not to harbor grudges

---

26 Brennan Manning, *The Ragamuffin Gospel* (Sister, OR: Multnomah Publishers, 1990), 34.

and to forgive seventy times seven. He tells us to pray for our enemies and to love those who spitefully use us.

If God keeps a ledger of our wrongs then He is not as loving as He demands us to be. If God doesn't forgive seventy times seven then why does God command us to? For some, God is more accountant than He is lover.

I know what some of you are thinking. What about hell? Isn't there a final judgment where humanity will be divided into sheep and goats? Aren't you ignoring a lot of scriptures that teach judgment as the consequence for our sins? A wise old preacher once said, "People who are preoccupied with hell and judgment generally have somebody else in mind."[27]

The scriptures clearly teach that God doesn't sentence anyone to hell. People choose hell when they reject God's love. Just like the father in Jesus's parable of the Prodigal Son, God allows us to make our choices and face the consequences of those choices. If we choose to live a self-centered or mediocre life, God lets us make that choice. However, because He loves us, He gives us all kinds of messages and warnings that our life is off track. Still, the choice is ours.

It is not God who punishes us when we make bad choices. We punish ourselves. It is not God who condemns us. Once again, the scriptures bear witness to this truth:

> *For God did not send his son into the world to condemn the world, but to save the world through him.*
> (John 3:17)

Some will never be convinced of God's unconditional love. They say things like, "What about the stories in the Bible where God mowed down entire armies, gave people leprosy, and told folks to kill their enemies, not to love them?" We get confused when we read the scripture backward. Every story in the Bible must now be interpreted in light of the Christ event. Jesus came to give us clearer understanding of what God is like. Sometimes we forget this.

---

27 Terence Grant, *The Silence of Unknowing: The Key to the Spiritual Life* (Liguori, MO: Liguori/Triumph, 1995), 68.

Terence Grant, in *The Silence of Unknowing,* offers some help here. He says:

> The ancient Israelites lived in a very violent time when war was necessary for a nation's survival. And so the Israelites, in their early understanding of God, interpreted God's fidelity to them in light of their situation: God's fidelity meant that God took their side in war. The underlying truth of these biblical stories is that God is always faithful, always with us. But in our Christian understanding, we know that God loves the Philistines as much as God loves the Israelites or anyone else.[28]

It's like one little child said in Sunday school, "God got sweeter when He learned from Jesus." I know it's hard to believe that God loves us no matter what. No one else ever has. And, since we don't believe such a love exists for us, we can never offer such a love to others.

Or can we?

CAN *WE* BE MERCIFUL?

When we truly accept our acceptance, when we truly believe we are loved unconditionally and forgiven, it radically changes how we view others and ourselves. How we treat each other is directly related to how we think God treats us. Knowing that God loves us unconditionally enables us to bring our painful failures to the surface where God can heal them.

We are much freer to express our guilt and shame in an atmosphere of love than we are in an atmosphere of fear. We can examine our dark side in a way we never could before if we believe we are loved and accepted. God is love, and those who live in Him must also live in love. Loving others is not a matter of willpower but of God's life and power flowing through us.

---

28 Ibid., 69.

We are only able to love because He first loved us (I John 4:19). Our love for one another is a channeling of God's love for us. We become conveyors of His amazing grace. In our own power, this command to be merciful is impossible. Our natural responses tend toward anger and revenge. The old "eye for an eye and tooth for a tooth" mentality is the only language our lower nature knows.

Our lower nature is incapable of producing mercy. Mercy comes from energy beyond the boundaries of our lower nature. It is completely spiritual. "Without me, you can do nothing," said Jesus. That includes being merciful. To really develop mercy, forgiveness, and compassion within ourselves, we must surrender ourselves to an infilling of divine mercy. William Barclay summarized "Blessed are the merciful" this way:

> O, the bliss that comes to the one who gets right inside the feelings of other people until he can see with their eyes, think with their feelings. He who does that will find that others do the same for him.[29]

Erma Bombeck shared an interesting observation about what it means to love with God's kind of love. She writes:

> It was one of those days when I wanted my own apartment—unlisted. My son was telling me, in complete detail, about a movie he had just seen, punctuated by 3000 "you knows?" My teeth were falling asleep. There were three phone calls—strike that—three monologues that could have been answered by a recording. I fought the urge to say, "It's been nice listening to you." And later, in the cab from home to the airport, I got another assault on my ear, this time by a cab driver rambling on about his son in college.
>
> At least there were thirty whole beautiful minutes before my plane took off, time for me to be alone with my own thoughts, to open a book and let my mind wander.

---

29 William Barclay, *The Gospel of Matthew*, vol. 1 (Philadelphia: The Westminster Press, 1975), 105.

A voice next to me belonging to an elderly woman said, "I'll bet it's cold in Chicago."

Stone-faced, I replied, "It's likely."

"I haven't been to Chicago in nearly three years," she persisted. "My son lives there."

"That's nice," I said, my eyes intent on my book.

"My husband's body is on this plane. We've been married 53 years. I don't drive, you know, and when he died a nun drove me home from the hospital. We aren't even Catholic. The funeral director let me come to the airport with him."

I don't think I have ever detested myself more than I did at that moment. Another human being was screaming to be heard and, in desperation, had turned to a cold stranger who was more interested in a novel than in the real-life drama at her elbow. She needed no advice, money, assistance, expertise, or even compassion—all she needed was someone to listen.

She talked numbly and steadily until we boarded the plane, then found her seat in the other section. As I hung up my coat, I heard her plaintive voice say to her seat companion, "I'll bet it's cold in Chicago."

I prayed, "Please, God, let her listen."[30]

Erma Bombeck knew that she had failed this woman. When one claims to be the son or daughter of a loving God, one loves as God loves. You listen as He listens. You touch as He touches. You care as He cares.

---

30 Erma Bombeck, "Please Listen!" Chicago *Sun-Times*, Feb. 26, 1977.

WILL WE BE MERCIFUL?

Edwin Markham, a poet, discovered, as he was about to retire, that the man to whom he had entrusted his financial portfolio had squandered all the money. Markham's dream of a comfortable retirement vanished overnight. For a while he gave in to anger, but one day while sitting at a table, Markham found himself drawing circles as he tried to soothe the storm within. Love finally had its way and he concluded: "I must forgive him, and I will forgive him."

Looking again at the circles he had been drawing he wrote these words:

> *He drew a circle to shut me out,*
> *Heretic, rebel, a thing to flout;*
> *But love and I had the wit to win,*
> *We drew a circle that took him in.*

Markham was the author of hundreds of poems but the words he wrote while forgiving are his most popular.

Great men and women of faith have always known that the act of forgiveness is divine and releases great healing power. The author and minister Charles Fillmore wrote that forgiveness is the most effective way of restoring inner harmony and balance. He said, "There is a mental treatment guaranteed to cure every ill that flesh is heir to: Sit for half an hour every night and forgive everyone against whom you have any ill will or antipathy." This doesn't happen automatically. It is a conscious choice.[31] There's an old French proverb that says, "To understand all is to forgive all." If we sought to understand at a deeper level, forgiveness would be much easier.

Eddie Long is pastor of New Birth Missionary Baptist Church in Atlanta, Georgia. Under his leadership the church has grown to 22,000 members. This pastor had trouble forgiving his father for the way he had been treated as a child. However, knowledge helped forgiveness grow:

---

31 See Victor M. Parachin, "Forgiveness: 10 Guidelines" in *The Big Book Bunch*, 7/4/2000.

My three brothers and I rarely talked with my father because of the resentment we felt toward him. My daddy was a strict disciplinarian, and we thought he did not love us. When Daddy suffered a stroke, I finally got up enough nerve to talk to him at the hospital. I was in my early thirties by then, but it still took a lot of courage for me to ask him this question while he was lying in bed: "Daddy, why did you treat us the way you did?"

Daddy looked up at me with tears in his eyes, and he began to describe his childhood. I did not know that my father had left home when he was only fourteen years old. Nor did I know that he had to raise all of his eight brothers and sisters by himself. He told me that his daddy stole his car, threw him out into the street, and took his money. I had no idea that my dad's father never hugged him.

My father cried as he told me what had happened to him, and immediately the Holy Ghost said, "Here is a seventy-year-old man who has been locked up for seventy years, not knowing any better and doing the best he can."

In that brief moment I received an instant release and I began to feel sorry for my dad. He had gone through life not knowing how to love my brothers and me, even though he wanted to. He did not know how to touch me. He wanted to but he could not.[32]

Being merciful means that we give the other person the benefit of the doubt. We choose to cooperate with God and give the person what the person needs, not what we may think the person deserves. God can work miracles when we trust the situation to Him.

You remember the story of Joseph. His wicked brothers faked his death and sold him into slavery. Years later, when Joseph could have had an easy revenge, he chose instead to love and forgive his brothers.

---

32 Eddie Long, *Called to Conquer* (Nashville: Thomas Nelson, 2000), 290.

How could he do that? He gave the situation to God and God used it to save a nation. Listen to what Joseph told his brothers: *But as for you, you meant evil against me; but God meant it for good, in order to bring it about as it is this day, to save many people.* (Genesis 50:20)

What about you? Are you grateful for the mercy God has shown you? Are you ready to begin sharing mercy with the ones who have hurt you? Someone has said, "He who will not forgive another destroys the bridge over which he himself must pass." It is true, what goes around does come around. In any situation we have a choice. Before we act or speak we should ask ourselves: *Is this what I really want in return?*

In *The Hiding Place*, Corrie ten Boom describes the suffering she went through in a German concentration camp during World War II. Against all odds, she survived that horrendous experience. When the war ended, she traveled extensively, speaking of how God's grace got her through those years.

Once, in the city of Munich, a man approached Corrie after she had finished speaking. She recognized him. He had been a prison guard in Ravensbrück and had been extremely cruel to her and her sister. He didn't remember that she had been in Ravensbrück and was telling Corrie that he had become a Christian.

He extended his hand to her and said, "Fräulein, how grateful I am for your message. To think that, as you say, He washed my sins away." All of a sudden Corrie's mind was flooded with horrible memories of this man. She struggled to raise her hand, but it remained at her side. She prayed, "Lord Jesus, forgive me and help me to forgive him." Nothing happened. Again she prayed, "Lord, I cannot forgive him. Forgive him through me."

She describes what happened next: "As I took his hand, the most incredible thing happened. From my shoulder along my arm and through my hand a current seemed to pass from me to him, while into my heart sprang a love that almost overwhelmed me."[33]

Will you pass God's forgiveness to others?

---

33 As cited in James W. Moore's *When You're a Christian, The Whole World Is From Missouri* (Nashville: Dimensions for Living, 1997), 33.

CHAPTER SIX

Owning My Shadow

Blessed are the pure in heart, for they shall see God.

—Matthew 5:8

Otis Campbell is one of the most lovable characters on *The Andy Griffith Show*. He has a problem but we love him anyway. His problem? He has a hard time resisting the temptation to drink too much.

We laugh at Otis because he's funny when he's intoxicated. But there is a downside to his lifestyle. In the episode called "Deputy Otis," we are given a little insight into how Otis really feels about his life.

Andy and Barney discover that Otis has been writing to his brother Ralph, telling him that he is a sheriff's deputy. Otis feels inferior and wants to make an impression on his brother, who is very respectable. Otis fools everyone until Ralph and his wife Verlaine decide to come to Mayberry for a visit.

Otis knows that he is in a fix, so he tells Andy about how he has deceived his brother for years. Feeling sorry for Otis, Andy offers to swear him in as a temporary deputy. Barney, as you can imagine, can't believe that Andy would even entertain such an idea. However, Andy insists, saying that Otis will be a deputy for only as long as his brother and sister-in-law are in town.

Ralph and Verlaine come to town and, for a while, Otis's charade works. Ralph even tries to tempt Otis to "have a snort" but Otis refuses. But before long, Otis's conscience begins to bother him, and he goes to the courthouse to tell Andy and Barney that they can stop pretending because the plan wasn't going to work.

While the three are talking, a funny but telling thing happens. Ralph, looking more like the old Otis, comes staggering in, gets the key, and locks himself up in a cell. Suddenly, the viewer sees that Otis is not the only town drunk in the family. Andy and Barney are amazed that *this* is the brother Otis is so worried about impressing.

Otis' reaction to his brother's drunkenness is the most interesting part of the story. He is disgusted and can't believe his brother would have such a flagrant disregard for the law. You see, Otis is looking at a mirror and doesn't like what he sees. For years Otis didn't want to admit he had a serious problem. With Andy's help, he even tried to cover his problem and act like all was well.

Otis eventually realized that covering his problem was impossible. Eventually, the truth will always come to the surface. Otis wasn't perfect, and he found that his brother Ralph wasn't perfect either. I wonder how their relationship as brothers might have been different had they just been honest with each other in the first place.

Joey Fann, in his wonderful book, *The Way Back to Mayberry*, sums up his take on this episode by saying:

> When you consider how we act around each other, you would think that we all have perfect lives.
>
> When we see each other, we talk about how great our jobs are going and how successful we have been.
>
> We tell each other that everything is fine and the family is doing great.
>
> We seem to be afraid to tell the truth because we will be perceived as having problems or not living up to expectations.

> If we were willing to share more, we would realize that our problems are not unique and, in fact, are very similar to the problems experienced by those around us.
>
> But this pressure to be perfect keeps our walls up, and we continue the façade. [34]

Admitting that we are not perfect is not easy. Like Otis, we fake it as long as we can. But sooner or later our shadow shows itself.

Robert Louis Stevenson's *The Strange Case of Dr. Jekyll and Mr. Hyde* brilliantly demonstrates that we have two distinct personalities sharing one body. One is good. One is not so good.

- Inside every puritan is a hedonist; inside every hedonist is a puritan; each denies the other.

- Inside every confident peacock is an insecure chicken; inside every chick is a peacock; each devalues the other.

- Inside every workhorse is a lazybones; inside every lazybones is a workhorse; each secretly envies the other.

- Inside each social butterfly is a lone wolf; inside each lone wolf is a social butterfly; each disdains the other.

- Inside every know-it-all is a questioner; inside each questioner is a know-it-all; each is impatient with the other.

- Inside each skillful person is a bluffer; inside each bluffer is a skillful person; each argues with the other.

- Inside each team player is a rebel; inside each rebel is a team player; each resents the other.

---

34 Joey Fann, *The Way Back to Mayberry: Lessons from a Simpler Time* (Nashville: Broadman and Holman Publishers, 2001), 78–79.

- Inside each rigid person is a sentimentalist; inside each sentimentalist is a rigid person; each disavows the other.

- Inside each believer is a doubter; inside each doubter is a believer; each rejects the other.[35]

The not-so-good part of us has many names: shadow, ego, old man, old nature, the flesh. This part of us is very competitive and feels that its very existence depends on being better than everyone else.

Our shadow nature loves to win and is always striving to do so. It wallows in its achievements, counts its awards, and brags about its superiority. It has to be better. It has to have more. It has to have its way, regardless.

On the other hand, there is a second person living in us called "spirit." It is our higher nature. Unlike the ego, our spirit is not interested in acquiring things or being better than anyone else. Spirit has no desire to defeat others. Spirit is not competitive. Spirit seeks one thing: love.

The Babemba tribe of South Africa demonstrates well the use of our higher nature. If a tribe member acts badly, he is placed at the center of the village. All work stops, and every man, woman, and child gathers, creating a large circle around the individual. Then they begin to address him, telling him and everyone in the circle about all the *good things* that individual has done in his life. No one is allowed to exaggerate or falsify his or her stories, nor is anyone allowed to be sarcastic. Sometimes this tribal ceremony can last for days, until every last positive comment is shared. When it is over, a huge celebration occurs and the individual returns to his tribal life.[36]

This tribe understands well the Apostle Paul's admonition: *Do not be overcome by evil, but overcome evil with good* (Romans 12:21). In

---

35 Dan Millman, *Everyday Enlightenment* (New York: Time Warner Books, 1998), 250.

36 This story was cited in a newsletter written by Peggy Haynes and is taken from Robin L. Silverman's *The Ten Gifts* (New York: St. Martin's Press, 2000).

order to overcome evil with good, we must acknowledge and own our shadow selves.

WE ALL HAVE A SMELLY REFRIGERATOR

I read of a couple who returned from a month-long trip to find a terrible odor throughout their house. It didn't take long to trace the odor to the refrigerator. Inside they discovered rotten food that had sat for weeks because of a power outage. It took days to scrub it down, clean it up, and air it out.

Human beings have a dark side just as smelly as this couple's refrigerator. It is that side of us that pulls us toward unhealthy, self-destructive behavior. Our shadow, our ego, our lower nature is what we want to insist we are not. However, like a smelly refrigerator, we need to own this part of ourselves if we are to enjoy spiritual health.

If this couple had dealt with their smelly refrigerator the way many of us deal with our shadow selves, our ego, our lower nature, they would have probably approached the situation in one of the following ways:

- They would realize that the stench was coming from the refrigerator, but instead of dealing directly with the source of the smell, they would repaint the outside of the refrigerator and spray heavy doses of air freshener around the house. When people would ask, "What's that awful smell?," they would look at them with wide-eyed innocence and reply, "What smell?" and spray more freshener.

- They would hire a contractor to wall off the offensive refrigerator in its own dark little room, and hope the smell didn't penetrate the walls.

- If all else failed, they would organize a community-wide campaign against the smelly refrigerator. They would express moral outrage over the threat that the refrigerator posed to public health.[37]

---

37 This illustration of the smelly refrigerator was taken from an article written by Patrick Means called "Dealing With Your Dark Side" and pub-

Repainting our exteriors and walling off our dark sides only postpones what has to be done. If we're going to be pure in heart, we've got to deal with our own smelly refrigerator. But how? Let me suggest three simple steps.

WE MUST ADMIT THAT
WE ALL HAVE A SMELLY REFRIGERATOR

Christians are mistaken in thinking that their dark side was eliminated at conversion. The sobering truth is Christians have a dark side that's every bit as active as those who are not Christian. Christians are just as capable of horrific deeds as anyone else.

Let a man whom God used greatly tell you about the power of the dark side. His name is Jim Bakker. The whole world knows what happened. This is what he said about it:

> When it was over, I quickly left the room, and in a daze, hurried to the elevator and pressed the button marking the eighth floor. The winter afternoon sun was already beginning to slide down on the horizon as I stepped inside my room. I was horrified. Oh, God! What have I done? I had not considered the consequences of my absurd attempt to make Tammy Faye jealous. I had not even paused to think of the potential ramifications of my actions while I was giving in to having sex with a woman other than my wife. I had simply reacted. I had opened the door to attack on the ministry I headed, my family, and me personally. Worse yet, the devil had not made me do any of it; I had done it of my own stubborn will. I disrobed and immediately stepped into the shower, turning the water on as hot as I could stand it. I never felt so dirty in all my life. Maybe if I make the water hotter, it will wash it all away, I thought.[38]

---

lished by the National Association of Christian Recovery, http://www.nacronline.com/recovery-issues/dealing-with-your-dark-side-part-1.

38 Jim Bakker, *I Was Wrong* (Nashville: Tyndale House Publishers, 1996), 21.

The Bible clearly teaches that despite Christ's work in our lives, we still remain a mix of light and dark, strength and weakness, until the day we die. To think otherwise is pure nonsense.

Jim Bakker's son, Jamie Charles, published a book called *Son of a Preacher Man.*[39] It is Jamie's account of what really happened behind the scenes during and after the scandal. The book is a sad commentary on how Christians treat Christians—especially how Christians treat Christians who fall into sin.

As you may remember, Jim Bakker was given the ridiculous sentence of forty-five years in prison—more than most murderers receive. And the sad thing is, most Christians didn't care. Jamie Charles led the campaign to get his father's sentence reduced but few Christian leaders offered their help.

Pat Robertson refused to take his calls even though Jim Bakker had been the creator and original host of Robertson's *The 700 Club.* Jamie Bakker claimed that Robertson was angry because his dad had refused to endorse his 1988 presidential bid.

Jamie Bakker called Oral Roberts and ended up talking with Oral's son, Richard. "Would you please help my dad?" he begged. "Would you help get my dad out of prison? Could you ask your people on TV to write letters to lower his sentence?" "No, I can't do that because I've got too many things to worry about," Richard Roberts answered.

Jamie even wrote to then-Vice President Al Gore asking for help in lowering his dad's prison sentence. He got no response. But one pastor took his call and offered assistance. You won't believe who it was. Jimmy Swaggart! One of the men who helped bring down Jim Bakker.

Jamie Bakker told Swaggart, "My dad's got a sentence hearing coming up. Would you write a letter to the parole board asking for my dad's sentence to be reduced?" Jamie fully expected Swaggart to say no. But he didn't. "Yes, I sure would." Swaggart responded.

---

39 Jay Bakker, *Son of a Preacher Man: My Search for Grace in the Shadows* (New York: HarperCollins, 2001).

Swaggart not only wrote the letter but went on national television and made this statement:

> I got a call the other day from Jim Bakker's sixteen-year-old son Jamie Charles, asking if I would help. This is what we've got to do. We've got to help this man get out of prison.[40]

I find that intriguing. The *good* people would not help, but the *bad* person did. Could it be that sinners who know they are sinners are more honest than Christians who think they aren't?

One pastor who tried his best to get his church to open its doors to recovery ministries was unsuccessful because some of his members resisted. They argued that recovery ministries attract too many chronically needy people. They wanted a church of normal people like themselves.

How many marriages could be better if the couple would own their shadow selves and admit that they have a smelly refrigerator in their relationship? One therapist was asked to tone down his lectures because in the words of the church's pastor, "If my couples have to admit to having problems, no one will come."

Today, what people need to hear is the truth, the whole truth, and nothing but the truth—and the truth is we are all fundamentally broken people.

There is a second step toward purity of heart.

WE MUST ADMIT THAT GOOD WORKS WON'T ELIMINATE OUR SHADOW SELVES

Most of us try to handle our lower nature by working harder. We have embraced the lie that we can work ourselves out of sinfulness. If we're spiritual enough, we think we will diminish our dark side. We even use good works to try to rid ourselves of our sinful nature: going to

---

40 Ibid., 108-112.

church, reading the Bible, and praying, for example. We think that these spiritual disciplines alone will transform our shadow selves.

If you remember your Greek mythology, you'll remember the myth of Sisyphus. Zeus punished him for his trickery by forcing him to roll a boulder to the top of a slope in Hades, only to have the boulder roll back down just as Sisyphus made it to the top. When we try to eliminate our lower nature, our shadow self, with good works, we create a similar plight for ourselves.

Like Sisyphus with his rock, we push ourselves uphill, hoping to make it to the top, only to fall back down to start the process all over again. The Apostle Paul knew this frustration all too well. He writes:

> *For I know that in me (that is, in my flesh) nothing good dwells for to will is present with me, but how to perform what is good I do not find. For the good that I will to do, I do not do; but the evil I will not to do, that I practice.* (Romans 7:18–19)

I know what you are thinking: Aren't we to strive to do good works? Aren't we to want to be better than we are? Aren't we to work hard to be more like Christ? Meister Eckhart, a German mystic, taught that spirituality is a matter of subtraction, not addition. True holiness is dropping the need to be somebody greater than we already are.

Jesus didn't try to be anybody important, did He? He refused that temptation and emptied Himself. The Bible admonishes us to follow His example:

> *Let the same mind be in you that was in Christ Jesus, who, though He was in the form of God, did not regard equality with God as something to be exploited, but emptied Himself, taking the form of a servant, being born in human likeness.* (Philippians 2:5–8)

We imitate Jesus by emptying ourselves of the notion that we have to work ourselves into a relationship with God. Remember poor old Otis? Did his hard work truly change him? No, it did not; not even with Andy's help.

This leads to the only real way to deal with our smelly refrigerator.

WE MUST ADMIT THAT WE ARE HELPLESS

No mere self-improvement course by itself stands a chance of taming or containing the restless energy of our lower nature, our shadow self. It takes the power of Christ. When we humble ourselves and confess that we are powerless, that, in turn, puts the responsibility for our recovery and spiritual health squarely on God and His grace.

How many days have been wasted in the vicious circle of sinning, feeling guilty, then beating ourselves up trying to get back into God's good graces, only to start the whole process over again as soon as we make our next mistake? Think about it. It's all so self-absorbed. It's sin-centered, not grace-centered.

Do you remember the story about the miraculous catch of fish in Luke's gospel (Luke 5:1–11)? The disciples had been fishing all night and had caught nothing. Jesus told them to cast their nets into the sea one more time.

A skeptical Peter reluctantly agreed to do so. The catch almost sunk the boat. It was a wonderful scene of God's power at work, but then Peter almost spoils it. He blurts out, "Lord, leave, I'm a sinful man." Jesus, however, paid little heed to Peter's words and merely told him not to be afraid.

It was as if Jesus was saying, "All right, Peter. You blew it, but it's okay. You're not the center of attention here. God's work is. So, acknowledge your lack of trust, learn from it, and move on. Let's not spoil the moment with excessive self-concern."[41]

The Kingdom doesn't revolve around us, or around how we feel, or think we should feel. The Kingdom of God is always God-centered. This fact requires that we change our whole way of looking at things.

---

41 See Terence Grant's *The Silence of Unknowing* (Liguori, MO: Liguori/ Triumph, 1995), 25.

This holds true in the area of repentance as well. We had better take ourselves out of the center of the meaning of "repentance"—otherwise we're just going to be in the way.

Barbara Taylor, a Christian preacher and writer, puts it very well:

> Repentance has nothing to do with feeling sorry— about yourself or for yourself. Repentance is not a matter of listing all the things you wish you had not done in your life and feeling badly about them, as if you could dilute them somehow with your regrets. Repentance is not about wishing you were a better person or keeping track of your faults, as if God might be persuaded to overlook them if only you could convince him that you are really, really sorry ... Repentance is not deciding to be nicer, or more generous, or more spiritual. It is not, for that matter, something that is under our control ...
>
> Repentance is more something that happens to you than something you decide ... repentance is a complete turnaround, a change of course, a change of heart and mind and life. Repentance is too busy redeeming the present to apologize for the past. Repentance spends less time hating the bad than loving the good. Repentance is a matter of being grasped by God, of being picked up and put down again so that everything looks different, so that you lose your old bearings and are offered new ones instead. That is God's part in the process, anyhow. Our part is to have the good sense to say "thank you" instead of "no" or "not yet," and to learn how to steer by those new lights instead of scrambling to return to our old familiar ones ...
>
> It is not, I think, something that happens only once. Life is full of such turning points, both large and small.[42]

---

42 Quoted in *Lectionary Homiletics*, vol. III, no. 1 (December 1991):14.

The greatest discovery that we will ever make is that the center of everything is not this little self of mine, but this *One who is unconditional love*; made known to us best in Jesus Christ, who loved us and gave Himself for us.

CHAPTER SEVEN

Peacemakers in Light of September 11, 2001

Blessed are the peacemakers, for they will be called sons of God.

—Matthew 5:9

How could you be human and not be furious at what happened on September 11, 2001? The sight of buildings burning on TV, smoke pouring out rows of windows, people jumping 1000 feet above the ground, choosing to jump rather than suffocate or burn to death.

There were unfortunate pedestrians struck and killed by objects, including bodies falling from planes or buildings above. Over 300 firemen lost their lives, including a 68-year-old fire department chaplain. The largest number of New York City firemen to have died in a single disaster before that week was twelve.

Search workers were finding arms, feet, teeth, but few intact bodies. Many families did not get anything back. The bodies of their loved ones had already been cremated by burning jet fuel. These poor families held funerals with empty boxes.

When I saw distraught Americans walking the streets of New York City, zombie-like, holding pictures of their missing loved ones, a part of me agreed wholeheartedly with *Time* magazine writer Lance Morrow.

In an article called "The Case for Rage and Retribution," Morrow argued:

> What's needed is a unified, unifying Pearl Harbor sort of purple fury—a ruthless indignation that doesn't leak away in a week or two. America needs to relearn a lost discipline, self-confident relentlessness—and to relearn why human nature has supplied us all with a weapon (abhorred in decent peacetime societies) called hatred.

Morrow continued:

> Anyone who does not loathe the people who did these things, and the people who cheer them on, is too philosophical for decent company.

> If what happened on Tuesday (September 11, 2001) does not give Americans the political will needed to exterminate men like Osama bin Laden and those who conspire with them in evil mischief, then nothing ever will and we are in for a procession of Black Tuesdays.[43]

I wish some of our religious leaders were as honest as Lance Morrow in expressing their indignation and rage over the evil done to this nation. Syrup-sweet sermons about loving your enemies is not what we need. As least I don't think so.

We need something else. We need truth, honest to God truth.

May I suggest,

IT'S OKAY TO BE ANGRY

In thinking about the horrendous evil that was perpetrated against our nation on September 11, 2001, righteous indignation is quite appropriate. How can we help but be angry? Anger is the normal human response. Anything other than anger would be abnormal.

---

43 Lance Morrow, "The Case for Rage and Retribution," *Time* Magazine, September 11, 2001.

For some reason, I keep thinking about the movie *The Patriot*. If you remember, Mel Gibson starred as Benjamin Martin, a reluctant revolutionary hero. Martin had an eighteen-year-old son named Gabriel who was eager to join the revolution. Gabriel's love for his country is revealed by one pastime: Throughout the first half of the movie, Gabriel diligently repairs an American flag that he had found in the dirt.

Tragically, Gabriel becomes a casualty of the war. Grieving deeply by the side of his dead son, Benjamin Martin appears ready to quit the cause. But Colonel Harry Burwell, a Continental Army officer, persuades him not to quit. Burwell recognizes that Benjamin Martin has great influence with the soldiers and his departure would demoralize the troops. In this moving scene, the colonel says, "Stay the course, Martin. Stay the course." But Benjamin Martin refuses, and the colonel rides away with his troops, leaving Martin behind.

Then something amazing happens. As Benjamin Martin is loading his son's personal effects on his horse, he finds the American flag Gabriel had successfully restored. As the dejected soldiers ride away, certain that they have seen the last of Benjamin Martin, Martin appears in the distance, carrying the flag. Riding upright in his saddle, face like flint, the stars and stripes whipping in the wind, Martin becomes a symbol of perseverance for the men of the Continental Army.

If ever our nation needed men and women like Benjamin Martin, it is now. Our anger is to be expected, but it must be channeled positively for the good of the world. Whether we are leaders at home or at school or at work or at church, we must never underestimate the power of our influence to rally others for the cause of law and order and goodness and decency.

The world is watching. Children are watching parents, students are watching teachers, congregations are watching their spiritual leaders. We, with faith and determination, must stay the course.

The Apostle Paul gave us good advice in dealing with the anger we feel. He said in Ephesians 4:26, *"Be angry but do not sin; do not let the sun go down on your anger, and do not make room for the devil."* This verse implies that being angry and sinning are not the same. The one doesn't necessarily lead to the other.

This leads me to a second thought:

IT'S OKAY TO BE ANGRY AT GOD

Admitting that you are angry at God means that you take your relationship with God seriously. I can assure you that He prefers honesty to pious pretense. If you're angry that He allowed this tragedy to occur, admit it. God commends, not condemns, our honesty.

Why is it okay to be angry at God? In his book *The Sins We Love: Embracing Brokenness, Hoping for Wholeness*, Randy Rowland gives one of the best answers I have ever heard:

> God is patient with us in the midst of our tomfoolery. Whether we sin with malicious intent or foolishly slip up, God is patient. I often shock people when I talk around the country by saying, "God isn't mad anymore. Any anger God may have had toward the human race was deposited in the God–Man, Jesus, on a cross two thousand years ago."
>
> People's jaws literally drop. Wow? God isn't mad? So many of us think God is standing around the corner, hidden and waiting to annihilate us for our most recent wrong. Yet, this misunderstanding of God is probably more offensive to God than the other sins we might commit. God isn't waiting to judge us. God is cheering for us and waiting to forgive us and reconcile with us. Paul's second letter to the Corinthian church says, "God chose not to hold our sins against us, but instead chose to become sin on our behalf in Jesus Christ so that you and I might be reconciled to God."[44]

---

44 Randy Rowland, *The Sins We Love: Embracing Brokenness, Hoping for Wholeness* (New York: Doubleday, 2000), 94.

The character of our loving God can become a model for us as we try to manage our anger. A God like the one Randy Rowland describes is a God with whom we can express the depth of our anger and hurt without fear of retaliation. Why do Christians sometimes feel angry toward God (whether we admit it or not)? One reason is that we are hurting and when we hurt, we look for someone to blame.

In John Updike's novel *Rabbit Run*, Harry Angstrom returns home one evening to find that his drunken wife has accidentally allowed their baby to drown in the bathtub. Heartbroken, Harry goes into the bathroom and kneels by the tub. He pulls the stopper out so easily. He groans, "How easy it was, yet with all the strength of heaven and earth, God did nothing. *Just that little stopper to lift.*"[45]

Too many good and faithful people have had to express that intense groan that wells up from deep within the soul. I've felt it myself. Why couldn't God have prevented the Hipps family from going to the place where our little daughter contracted the virus that ended her life at the age of four?

I'm sure my comments are making some of you uncomfortable. Why? Probably because good religious people can't stand to have other good religious people confess that they are, or have been, angry with God. I think of poor old Job. He did not deserve that much heartache. Neither did the tens of thousands of Americans who woke up September 12, 2001.

I join others in expressing shame and outrage at the words of Jerry Falwell, who said the following on national television:

> "I really believe that the pagans, and the abortionists and the feminists, and the gays and lesbians who are actively trying to make that an alternative lifestyle, the ACLU, People for the American Way, all of them who have tried to secularize America—I point a finger in their face and say 'You helped this happen.'"

---

45 As cited in M. Craig Barnes, *Hustling God: Why We Work So Hard for What God Wants to Give* (Grand Rapids: Zondervan, 1999), 131.

God forgive our ministers for saying such stupid things. If God would do such awful things to people just to teach those who survive a lesson, then we're all in trouble. Who's to say you aren't the next object lesson?

Jerry Falwell, to his credit, did retract his original statement and offer an apology. In a letter to *USA Today* he wrote:

> On September 13, during an appearance of *The 700 Club*, in the midst of the shock and mourning of a dark week for America, I made a statement that I should not have made and that I sincerely regret. I apologize that, during a week when everyone appropriately dropped all labels and no one was seen as liberal or conservative, Democrat or Republican, religious or secular, I singled out for blame certain groups of Americans. In doing so, I misstated my personal and deeply held belief that no one is to blame for the barbaric happenings of September 11 except the hijackers and terrorists. Blaming any American or group of Americans was wrong and was not my intent.

> Obviously, neither I, nor anyone else, have any reason to believe that the terrorist-inflicted atrocities of September 11 have anything to do with the judgment of God, and I should not have stated otherwise.

> Our Lord is a God of love. He proved it ultimately and forever when He sent His Son, Jesus Christ, to die on the cross for all sinners, including me.

> None of us understands why bad things sometimes happen to good people, but, as the Rev. Billy Graham recently stated so well, this is where our faith must take over.

> My statements were understandably called divisive. This grieves me.

As a pastor for 45 years, my sincere desire in this tragedy is to provide love, prayers and comfort for all of the victims and their families. On September 13 I failed.

The Rev. Jerry Falwell,
Chancellor, Liberty University,
Senior Pastor, Thomas Road Baptist Church
Lynchburg, VA.[46]

Back to admitting that at times we can be angry with God. Michele Novotni and Randy Petersen in their book, *Angry With God*, offer some excellent suggestions.

- Give yourself permission to openly express your feelings to God. Don't feel guilty about being angry with Him; He knows that it's natural to sometimes wrestle with hard emotions. Realize that God already knows you're angry with Him, so there's no need to hide it. Know that He will welcome communication from you about your anger, since He wants to keep building a closer relationship with you every day, and part of developing a bond is sharing deep feelings.

- Understand that your perspective on any situation is limited, but God's perspective is unlimited. Ask God questions if you'd like. He may choose to answer them.

- Consider whether your ideas about God, and your expectations of Him, align with biblical truth about Him. For example, God doesn't cause suffering (which is a result of humans' fall), but He sometimes allows it if it can accomplish a greater purpose in your life. God always has your best interests at heart, even in the middle of hard experiences. Study Scripture to discover more about who He is and how He works, and pray for the Holy Spirit to help you internalize what you find.

---

46 *USA Today*, September 21, 2001.

- When approaching God about a particular grievance, confess your anger (without worrying that God will view you as unfaithful for doing so), explain why you're angry, listen for whatever responses God may offer you, and release the physical energy generated by your anger in ways that help you, such as screaming, punching a pillow, or playing sports.

- After you've expressed your anger and listened to God's response, reevaluate the situation that caused you to become angry with Him. Consider it in light of whatever response you may have heard from God, or new information you've discovered about God's character, or simply your decision to surrender your anger and trust Him.

- Seek to restore a positive relationship with God in prayer by letting Him know that you're no longer holding a grudge toward Him and are open to following Him as He continues to lead you each day.

- Take note of all the positive ways God is working in your life, and thank Him for those blessings.[47]

I've said it's okay to be angry. It's even okay to be angry at God.

Now I want to say:

IT'S *NOT* OKAY TO IGNORE THIS BEATITUDE

During our years as missionaries in Brazil, the Archbishop of the Catholic Church there was a man named Don Helder Camara. He led the Catholic Church during some of the most difficult years in Brazilian history.

In 1999 he visited a church in Berkeley, California, where he answered questions about his life and ministry. Someone asked, "After facing death squads, would-be assassins, corporations oppressing the

---

47 Adapted from *Angry With God* by Michele Novotni and Randy Peterson (Colorado Springs: Pinon Press, 2001).

poor, violent government opposition, and even hostile forces within your own church, who is your most difficult opponent?"

Not saying a word, Don Helder pointed his hand into the air, slowly arched it around until it turned on himself, his index finger pointing to his heart. "I am my own worst enemy," he said, "my most difficult adversary. Here I have the greatest struggle for peace."[48]

When Jesus said, "Blessed are the peacemakers," He knew that if we want to make peace with others, we need first to be at peace with ourselves. Before we can work for peace, we must have a peaceful heart.

Think about it. Even if we transported all of Earth's bombs to the moon, the reason for war and bombs would still be here in our hearts and minds. It wouldn't be long until we would make new bombs.[49]

What does the Bible, God's word, actually teach us about peace? The Hebrew word *shalom* isn't easy to translate into English because of the depth and breadth of its connotations. Actually, it possesses no single meaning, though most scholars translate it as *completeness*, *soundness*, or *wholeness*. To be sure, it extends far beyond "peace," as we commonly think of it in the English language.[50]

In Hebrew, *shalom* means the end of war and conflict, but it also means friendship, contentment, security, health, prosperity, abundance, tranquility, harmony, and even salvation. That's the kind of peace Jesus says we're to make as Christians—even if we're angry and don't want to.

In his book, *He Is Our Peace*, Howard Goeringer suggests an even more radical meaning of shalom: *love of one's enemies*. Jerusalem was invaded by Babylon in 600 BC. The Babylonians carried away many hostages and, in such trying times, the prophet Jeremiah wrote these

---

48 See John Dear's *Living Peace: A Spirituality of Contemplation and Action* (New York: Random House, 2001), 9.
49 Thich Nhat Hanh in Johann Christoph Arnold's *Seeking Peace: Notes and Conversation Along the Way* (Farmington, PA: The Plough Publishing House, 1998), xii.
50 Ibid, p. 13

remarkable words to those in exile in Babylon: *Seek the shalom of the city where I have sent you into exile, and pray to the Lord on its behalf, for in its shalom you will find your shalom.* (Jeremiah 29:7)

Goeringer writes:

> As we might expect, Jeremiah's letter was not popular, not a bestseller. The suffering hostages could not see how their well-being and the well-being of their captors were inseparably bound together. To think of serving their captors in a spirit of kindness, nursing their sick, teaching their children Jewish games, working an extra hour for them! This was utter foolishness.[51]

These were hard words for those captive Jews to hear. They are difficult words for hurting Americans to hear too. This beatitude does not say, "Blessed are the peace*lovers*," or "Blessed are the peace*keepers*." It says, "Blessed are the peace*makers*."

Stephen Crotts offers a concrete example as to what peacemaking entails.

> Consider a common pot of violets on your household windowsill. A bit parched, starting to brown, they haven't bloomed in two years. So you determine to be a peacemaker for them.

> First, you have to take away the harmful things. A dog chews on them. Kids knock the pot off the sill. It's too cold or too hot where it sits. So you remove these threats. But you still haven't created shalom.

> For you must add the presence of helpful things. Sunlight in the correct amount. Moisture. Fertilizer. Pruning. And in four months the pot of violets is

---

51 Howard Goeringer, *He Is Our Peace: Meditation on Christian Non-Violence,* (Farmington, PA: Plough Publishing House, 1994), 18.

a verdant, blooming beauty. You are a successful peacemaker.[52]

Like it or not, peacemaking is a major part of our ministry as Christians. We are summoned by the Prince of Peace to dedicate ourselves to anything that contributes to human wholeness. The hope of our great nation is not in our military might. Our hope is not the coalition of nations rushing to our aid. Our hope *is* printed on our coins, "In God We Trust."

A week after those horrendous attacks on 9/11 a powerful prayer by pastor and author Max Lucado circulated throughout the United States and the world via the Internet:

Dear Lord,

We're still hoping we'll wake up. We're still hoping we'll open a sleepy eye and think, "What a horrible dream."

But we won't, will we, Father? What we saw was not a dream. Planes did gouge towers. Flames did consume our fortress. People did perish. It was no dream and, dear Father, we are sad.

There is a ballet dancer who will no longer dance and a doctor who will no longer heal. A church has lost her priest; a classroom is minus a teacher. Cora ran a food pantry. Paige was a counselor and Dana, dearest Father; Dana was only three years old. (Who held her in those final moments?)

We are sad, Father. For as the innocent are buried, our innocence is buried as well. We thought we were safe. Perhaps we should have known better. But we didn't.

---

52 Stephen M. Crotts, *The Beautiful Attitudes: The Wisdom of the Beatitudes* (Lima, OH: CSS Publishing, 1996), 66.

And so we come to you. We don't ask you for help; we beg you for it. We don't request it; we implore it. We know what you can do. We've read the accounts. We've pondered the stories and now we plead, "Do it again, Lord. Do it again."

Remember Joseph? You rescued him from the pit. You can do the same for us. Do it again.

Remember the Hebrews in Egypt? You protected their children from the angel of death. We have children too, Lord. Do it again.

And Sarah? Remember her prayers? You heard them. Joshua? Remember his fears? You inspired him. The women at the tomb? You resurrected their hope. The doubts of Thomas? You took them away. Do it again, Lord. Do it again.

You changed Daniel from a captive into a king's counselor; you took Peter the fisherman and made him Peter an apostle. Because of you, David went from leading sheep to leading armies. Do it again, Lord, for we need counselors today, Lord. We need apostles. We need leaders. Do it again, Lord.

Most of all do again what you did at Calvary. What we saw here last Tuesday, you saw there that Friday. Innocence is slaughtered. Goodness murdered. Mothers weeping. Evil dancing. Just as the smoke eclipsed our morning, so the darkness fell on your Son. Just as our towers were shattered, the very Tower of Eternity was pierced.

And by dusk, heaven's sweetest song was silent, buried behind a rock. But you did not waver, O Lord. You did not waver. After three days in a dark hole, you rolled the rock again, Lord. Grant us a September Easter.

We thank you, dear Father, for these hours of unity. Christians are praying with Jews. Republicans are standing with Democrats. Skin colors have been covered by the ash of burning buildings. We thank you for these hours of unity.

And we thank you for these hours of prayer. The Enemy sought to bring us to our knees and succeeded. He had no idea, however, that we would kneel before you. And he has no idea what you can do.

Let your mercy be upon our President, Vice President, and their families. Grant to those who lead us wisdom beyond their years and experience. Have mercy upon the souls who have departed and the wounded who remain. Give us grace that we might forgive and faith that we might believe.

And look kindly upon your church. For two thousand years you've used her to heal a hurting world.

Do it again, Lord. Do it again.

Through Christ, Amen.

CHAPTER EIGHT

Happy Are the Harassed

Blessed are those who are persecuted because of righteousness, for theirs is the kingdom of heaven. Blessed are you when people insult you, persecute you and falsely say all kinds of evil against you because of me.

—Matthew 5:10–11

After England had colonized the country of India they yearned for recreation and decided to build a golf course in the city of Calcutta. Upon completion of the golf course the English were presented with a unique obstacle. Monkeys would drop out of the trees, run across the course, and steal the golf balls. The monkeys would play with the balls for a few minutes then toss them here and there.

The English did everything in their power to control these harassing monkeys. They built high fences around the fairways and greens, but no fence is a challenge to an ambitious monkey. Next, the English golfers tried coaxing the monkeys away from the course. However, the little monkeys found nothing as entertaining as watching humans jump up and down whenever their little white balls were disturbed.

Then the British began trapping the monkeys, but for every monkey they carried off, another one would appear to take its place. Final solution? The English golfers knew they were powerless to control the monkeys so they made a new rule: *Play the ball where the monkey drops it.*

How would you like to play golf on that course in Calcutta? You make a beautiful drive down the center of the fairway only to have a monkey grab it and drop it in the rough. Or, the opposite could happen. You hook or slice it only to have a monkey grab it and drop it two feet from the cup.

If you think about it, playing golf on this course in India is very similar to what we experience in life. Sometimes the monkeys are good to us, sometimes they aren't. We all have to play the game from where the ball is dropped.[53]

Let's talk about one of the most irritating monkeys on the course of life. His name is *persecution.*

WHAT IS PERSECUTION?

In the giving of the beatitudes, Jesus saved his toughest teaching for last: *Blessed are those who are persecuted for righteousness' sake.* Persecution is something that every Christian will have to face. Perhaps you don't know this, but more Christians have been killed in the last 100 years than in the previous 1900 years combined.

On September 28, 1997, M. Craig Barnes, pastor of the National Presbyterian Church, Washington DC, preached a powerful sermon on the persecuted church. He began his message with this vivid picture:

> One evening the soldiers talked about a girl they had raped many times in the course of the afternoon. Through it all, the girl sang hymns, strange evangelical songs, and she kept on singing, even after they shot her in the chest. She lay on the ground with the blood flowing from her chest, but she kept on singing—a bit weaker than before, but still singing. Then the soldiers

---

53 See Gregory Knox Jones's *Play the Ball Where the Monkey Drops It: Why We Suffer and How We Can Cope_*(New York: HarperCollins, 2001), 3–5.

grew tired of this and shot her again, but still she sang. And then the soldiers became afraid. Terrified of the girl, they fell upon her with machetes, and at last the singing stopped.

For the last two thousand years, someone has always been trying to stop the singing of Christ's followers. The report I just read sounds a lot like the accounts of early church persecution I studied in history books. But this report does not come from a history book. It comes from *The New Yorker* magazine (December 6, 1993), and it describes contemporary events.[54]

We Christians in the West have had the monkey drop the ball near the cup for a long time. On September 11, 2001, the ball was dropped in the rough. It has been brought home to us that there are non-Christians willing to lay down their lives in order to kill as many people as possible that do not subscribe to their beliefs. The game is not going to be as easy as it used to be. And why should it be?

Our Lord Jesus suffered much persecution during His life and ministry, even to the point of being executed. The same is true of His disciples. Tradition tells us:

- James, the son of Zebedee, was beheaded in Jerusalem, the first of the apostles to die, during the Easter season in about the year AD 44.

- Matthew was slain with the sword in a city in Ethiopia.

- Mark was dragged through the streets of Alexandria until he expired.

- Luke was hanged on an olive tree in Greece.

- James the Less was thrown from a pinnacle or wing of the temple.

---

54 Robert J. Morgan, *Nelson's Complete Book of Stories, Illustrations, and Quotes* (Nashville: Thomas Nelson Publishers, 2000), 760.

- Philip was hanged up against a pillar in Phrygia.

- Bartholomew was flayed alive.

- Andrew was scourged then tied to a cross where he preached to the people for two days before dying.

- Jude was shot to death with arrows.

- Thomas was run through the body with a lance.

- Simon Zelotes was crucified.

- Peter was crucified upside down.

- Matthias was stoned and beheaded.

- John was exiled to the penal island of Patmos and later became the only apostle to die a natural death.[55]

The persecution of which Jesus warns is not limited to martyrdom. Persecution presents itself in a variety of ways. In free countries we can suffer a different kind of persecution because persecution wears many faces. At one time or another every Christian will be snubbed, rejected, discriminated against, or harassed. Calculated insults and contrived put-downs can be weapons wielded even by religious people against their own kind.[56]

Peer pressure can be a powerful form of persecution. Christian high school students face it every day of their lives. If you live by high ideals, your faith stance will be challenged. Our Christian lifestyle is going to rub against the grain of the value system around us. As a matter of fact, if the way you live doesn't rub against the grain of a Christ-less world, then something is wrong with you. The light of Christ in you will expose the darkness in others. And you should brace yourself, because most will lash out at the source of their discomfort.

Paul Little told about being in a golf game with Billy Graham, another Christian, and an unbeliever. As the game wore on, the non-

---

55 Ibid., 763.
56 Robert Schuller, *The Be Happy Attitudes: Eight Positive Attitudes That Can Transform Your Life* (Dallas: Word Publishing, 1985), 209–210.

Christian became more and more irritated. After a while he snapped at Paul Little and said something to this effect: "I don't need Billy Graham preaching at me."

The truth of the matter is that Billy Graham had not said one negative or accusing word that day. There had been no conversation about spiritual matters nor had Billy Graham tried to convert the individual. He had just had a good time playing golf. It was the light in him that spoke. You see, light dispels darkness. At times it confronts and convicts *nonverbally*.

This may surprise you but there is an even more sinister form of persecution called self-persecution. When we fail to live up to our own expectations, we often persecute ourselves. Isn't that sad? Excessive regret, guilt, and remorse can torture the soul. Self-recrimination is perhaps the most prevalent and widespread form of persecution.

There was a medical school administrator named Mr. Barwick who had a serious circulation problem in his leg but refused amputation. Finally, the pain became so great Mr. Barwick said, "I'm through with that leg. Take it off."

Shortly before the surgery began Barwick asked his doctor, "What do you do with legs after they are removed?" "Usually we incinerate them," replied the doctor. Barwick, surprising everyone within earshot, said, "I want to preserve my leg in a pickling jar. I'm going to place it on my mantle, sit in my armchair, and taunt that leg saying, 'Hah! You can't hurt me anymore!'"

Ultimately Barwick got his wish, but the despised leg had the last laugh. Barwick began to suffer phantom limb pain of the worst degree. He could feel the torturing pressure of cramped muscles that throbbed and itched even after the wound had healed.

Commenting on Mr. Barwick's dilemma, Dr. Paul Brand said, "He had hated the leg with such intensity that the pain had unaccountably lodged permanently in his brain." Brand added, "To me, phantom limb pain provides wonderful insight into the phenomenon of false guilt. Christians can be obsessed by the memory of some sin committed years ago and it never leaves them, crippling their ministry, their devotional lives, and their relationships with others. Unless they experience the truth of 1 John 3:19–20 that 'God is greater than our conscience,' they became as pitiful as poor Mr. Barwick, shaking his fist in fury at the pickled leg on the mantel."[57]

OUR RESPONSE TO PERSECUTION

According to this beatitude, when persecution comes our way, we should *Rejoice and be glad.* A good example of this type of attitude is found in Acts 5. If you remember, the apostles were preaching and performing mighty works of God near the temple area. In anger and jealousy, the high priest arrested the apostles and had them thrown in jail.

While in prison an angel appeared and released them. They went back to the temple and once again began preaching. When the religious authorities discovered their escape, they apprehended them again, this time giving them a terrible flogging.

How did these apostles respond to their persecution? The Bible says, *So they went on their way from the presence of the Council, rejoicing that they had been considered worthy to suffer shame for His name. And every day, in the temple and from house to house, they kept right on teaching and preaching Jesus as the Christ.* (Acts 5:41–42)

Accepting persecution, playing from where the monkey drops the ball, is not easy. But it is required if we're to be like Jesus. Jesus played from where the monkey dropped the ball. When at the cross, persecuted by the Roman centurion, He did not lash back at the man, nor did He threaten him. Instead, He prayed, "Father, forgive them all." When we respond in love, light overcomes darkness. How do we know this? The same centurion proclaimed hours later, *"Surely, this was the Son of God"* (Matthew 27:54). We can choose to live in victory regardless of our circumstances. We do not have to answer evil with evil. When persecuted, we can choose the higher road.

---

57 Morgan, *Nelson's Complete Book*, 306–307.

Dr. Viktor Frankl, author of *Man's Search For Meaning*, was a living example of choosing the higher road. Dr. Frankl, a Jew, lost his wife, his children, and his parents in the Holocaust. On one occasion the Nazis stripped him naked. They noticed that he still had on his wedding ring and demanded that he remove it.

As he handed the ring to his persecutors, he said to himself, "You can take away my wife, you can take away my children, you can strip me of my clothes and freedom, but there is one thing no person can ever take away from me—and that is my freedom to choose how I will react to what happens to me."[58] How about you? Do you believe, like Dr. Frankl, that we are free to choose our attitude in any given situation—to maintain an attitude of faith, no matter how negative our circumstance?

There was a politician who had done the best job he could, yet he was severely criticized by the news media. Depressed and exhausted he drove to the country to visit a friend who happened to be a farmer.

Sitting on the porch one night the politician said to his farmer friend, "What am I going to do? I have tried so hard and there are some who seem to enjoy criticizing me." Not far from where they were sitting the farmer's dog was barking at the moon. Taking advantage of this opportunity, the farmer said to his friend, "See my old dog barking at the moon? He'll keep barking and the moon will keep on shining. You keep on shining regardless of who's barking!"[59]

OUR REWARD FOR ENDURING THE PERSECUTION

Mark's gospel offers this incredible promise:

> *Assuredly, I say to you, there is no one who has left house or brothers or sisters, or father or mother or wife or children or lands, for my sake and the gospel's,*
>
> *Who shall not receive a hundredfold now in this time—house and brothers and sisters and mothers and*

---

58 Schuller, *Be Happy Attitudes;* 212–213.
59 Ibid., 216–217.

> *children and lands, WITH PERSECUTIONS—and in*
> *the age to come, eternal life.* (Mark 10:29–30)

Did you catch that? A boatload of blessings but "with persecutions." That sounds very much like playing the ball where the monkey drops it; taking the good with the bad.

We also can be comforted in knowing that our suffering as Christians won't go on forever. *Weeping may endure for a night, but joy cometh in the morning* (Psalm 30:5). Paul reminded the Corinthians that persecution is never permanent: *For our light affliction, which is but for a moment, worketh for us a far more exceeding and eternal weight of glory* (II Corinthians 4:17). Let us remember that, by his grace, God can overwhelm that which was meant to harm us and use it for good.

Have you ever wondered why Jesus sent the blind man to the Pool of Siloam to wash his eyes? Jesus could have just said, "Be healed," and the man's sight would have come to him on the spot. But Jesus wanted the man to do something, to exercise obedience, so He sent him to the Siloam Pool to wash his eyes. But there's an interesting little detail to the story. Before sending him off, Jesus smeared mud on his eyelids. Why? Why would Jesus do this? The mud provided the motivation for the obedience Christ required.

We don't always understand why mud gets in our eyes, but sometimes if it weren't there, we would never bring critical areas of our lives into obedience to Jesus Christ. And without obedience, the work of God can never be displayed in us. God, in His infinite grace and wisdom, sometimes uses mud to restore our sight.[60]

And we must trust that wherever the monkey drops the ball, God will help us play the rest of the game with grace and dignity. Then one good day, we're going to hit a hole in one and the monkeys will scamper, unable to harm or help us.

John Claypool tells of hearing Fred Craddock preach on the sixteenth chapter of Romans. As you may know, this chapter is largely a listing of names. St. Paul is writing to the church in Rome and he's

---

60 Morgan, *Nelson's Complete Book*, 747.

asking to be remembered to a variety of individuals whose lives have been linked to his somewhere in the past.

Dr. Craddock invited all those in the service to get out their bulletins and write down the names of the people most beloved to them. He then instructed them to carry that list with them in the future and to add names to it as the circle of their affection grew.

He went on to say, "When you die, take the list with you into the next life." Then he said, "I know when you get to heaven's gate, St. Peter will stop you and say, 'Look, you can't bring anything with you from the other life. Let me have that piece of paper.' And you will probably say, 'Oh, it's really not anything. It's just a list of people whom I have loved and who have loved me across the years.'

"And St. Peter will say, 'Can I look at it?' And you will stand on one foot and then the other and say, 'Oh, these names wouldn't mean anything to you.' But St. Peter will insist, and you will finally hand over the list."

Then Craddock concluded by saying that St. Peter will take that list and begin to read it: "Frank, Susan, George, Bill, Ophelia," and then a great smile will break across his face, and he will say, "Do you know what? When I was walking over to work this afternoon, I saw these very people. They were making a poster. It had your name on it, and it said, 'Welcome Home!'"[61]

---

61   John R. Claypool, *God Is an Amateur* (Cincinnati, OH: Forward Movement Publication, 1994), 66–67.

Epilogue

Looking in the Rearview Mirror

Not long ago a church member's mother from North Carolina visited our church here in Tennessee. When I introduced myself she asked, "Pastor, do you remember a woman named Lois Pendley?" I said, "Yes, I do. She was a member of my very first pastorate." "Well," the lady said, "She is now in a nursing home severely challenged with dementia. However, she speaks often of 'her' pastor, Richard Hipps. I thought you would want to know that."

Thirty-four years ago, as a college student, I became this precious woman's pastor. Lois Pendley and two hundred other brave souls risked calling a ministerial student with no experience to be their pastor. For five years, they helped shape my life and ministry.

Being humbled by the fact that Lois Pendley, in her challenged state, was remembering me as "her" pastor, I sat down, got comfortable, and relived as many memories as possible. I took my time and not only remembered people and places, I also asked the Holy Spirit to help me interpret what I was remembering. It was truly amazing, a deeply spiritual exercise. One thought rose to the top of all these memories: God loves me and God is always faithful.

I have no idea how God has used my life and ministry over the years, but hearing about Lois Pendley gave me a glimpse. I think one of the joys (and surprises) of heaven will be seeing how our small stories help enrich God's big story. Perhaps it will be just a paragraph or a sentence or a phrase but, just the same, God's big story is incomplete without God's working in our small stories.

Even though it is heartbreaking to watch age or dementia claim a loved one's mind, it is a mistake to think that disease destroys a person's desire or ability to worship. I have known many individuals who lose their ability to recall facts and events as they previously could, but who remember such matters of faith as a pastor's name, the Lord's Prayer, or a hymn. Although our loved ones and friends may forget many things, God has not forgotten them.

I could confess that I do not have a problem with memory because I do not have dementia, but there are not many of us who do not struggle with memory problems. Most of us have selective memory, especially when it suits our needs. We have memory problems constrained by time and interest. We are too busy to sift through our past and remember the prints left on our hearts by others and be grateful. We are often too absorbed in other ways to remember the people who gave us chances and were living models of God's faith in us.

As I thought of Lois Pendley and all the people who allowed me to share in the sacred places of their lives, I recalled the words to an old hymn "Come Thou Fount of Every Blessing," especially the line "Here I raise mine Ebenezer." An Ebenezer is a memorial stone, similar to the one erected by God's people in Joshua 4 to remember God's presence and participation in their lives.

One of the greatest enemies of faith is forgetfulness. Holy Spirit-inspired remembrances of the past can encourage attitudes and behavior in the present. When we discipline ourselves to remember, deeply remember, it can remind us of our many blessings, spur us on, and keep us focused. The remembering can form our hearts and help us live and tell the Story of God's love.

What would happen if we each raised our own Ebenezer by recalling year by year as many memories as possible and the ways we witnessed God present and participating in and through our lives? The look in the rearview mirror would probably encourage each of us to trust God more and declare God's faithfulness daily. And, it would help us never forget the benefits of living a focused life.

> *This I recall to mind,*
> *Therefore I have hope.*
> *The Lord's loving kindness never ceases,*
> *For His compassions never fail.*
> *They are new every morning;*
> *Great is your faithfulness.* (Lamentation 3:21–23)